A VAIN CONCEIT

A VAIN CONCEIT

BRITISH FICTION IN THE 1980s

D. J. TAYLOR

BLOOMSBURY

First published in Great Britain 1989

Copyright © 1989 D. J. Taylor

Bloomsbury Publishing Ltd, 2 Soho Square, London W1V 5DE

A CIP catalogue record for this book is
available from the British Library.

ISBN 0 7475 0475 X

10 9 8 7 6 5 4 3 2 1

Phototypeset by Rowland Phototypesetting Ltd,
Bury St Edmunds, Suffolk
Printed and bound in Great Britain by
Richard Clay Ltd, Bungay, Suffolk

CONTENTS

RACHEL'S

ACKNOWLEDGEMENTS

Parts of this book originally appeared in a slightly different form in the following newspapers and periodicals: *The Independent, Sunday Times, Guardian, Private Eye, London Evening Standard, Panurge* and *The Spectator*. I am grateful to their respective editors and publishers for permission to reprint copyrighted material.

Several people provided valuable suggestions for the Appendix. I am grateful in particular to Marcus Berkmann, Mark Everett, Sebastian Faulks, Tim Jenks and John Walsh.

Until one has some kind of professional relationship with
books one does not discover how bad the majority of them are.

George Orwell, *Confessions of a Book Reviewer*

Some Italian once wrote that the critic secretly wants to kill
the writer. Is that true? Up to a point. We all hate golden
eggs. Bloody golden eggs again, you can hear the critics mutter
as a good novelist produces yet another good novel; haven't
we had enough omelettes this year?

Julian Barnes, *Flaubert's Parrot*

I

The Decline of the English Novel

It is true to say that in the past most English critics have
been fortified by the idea, whether explicitly formulated or
not, that by right of birth they are the guardians and
interpreters of one of the world's great literary traditions.
Put that bluntly, it may make them sound as though they
were the custodians of the Crown Jewels, and no doubt a
good deal of inferior criticism has often been a form of
patriotic advertising.

John Gross, *The Rise and Fall of the Man of Letters*

The publishing industry, like the Labour Party or the Church
of England, exists forever in a state of crisis. Like the Labour
Party and the Church of England it periodically produces
bulletins on its own shaky state of health. The 1970s was a
particularly fertile decade for the public reckoning-up of balance sheets and gloomy pondering over trends: a time of
general economic uncertainty, it was also a time of specific
and unprecedented pressure on an industry hitherto insulated
by stable prices and – in the matter of library supply – unac-
knowledged subsidy. The price of a hardback novel, which
had fallen steadily in real terms for nearly a century, doubled
in the early 1970s. A book which in 1972 cost you £2 would
have retailed at £3.95 in 1976. Libraries, their budgets frozen
or reduced by cost-conscious local authorities, cut back on
the purchase of new books. Paper and printing costs soared.
The response to this 'publishing crisis' (an early issue of
Granta appeared under the then optimistic banner of 'Beyond

the Publishing Crisis') was characteristically circumspect. Not many people went bankrupt, but a number of fiction lists got scrapped, and it was at all times possible to earn a few pounds in one of the weekly magazines by writing an article on 'The Death of Literature'.

The general air of malaise which infected the 1970s, an uncertainty detectable in nearly every area of public life, turns up repeatedly in the decade's books about books; a genre which no decade has ever been able to do without. It hangs over J. A. Sutherland's *Fiction and the Fiction Industry*, which confined itself to the novel, and is a staple of Per Gedin's *Literature in the Marketplace*, a famously gloomy book by a Swedish publisher convinced not so much of the decline of the novel as of the crack-up of Western civilization. With hindsight – *economic* hindsight – the critic can scoff at this accumulation of woe. Its thesis will be familiar to anyone who has ever dipped into a copy of the *Bookseller*. There are too many books chasing too few readers; the international conglomerates are squeezing out the chaps in Bloomsbury; we are being deluged with trash; the libraries spend only a tithe of their reduced income on filling the shelves. In other words, see any book trade anatomist since Ernest Rhys.

It is easy to laugh. There is a sense in which publishers' reflections on the state of trade have consistently resembled farmers' complaints about the weather. The skies open. The rain falls, and yet – curiously – the crops are still harvested and everyone manages to make ends meet. But at the time the despondency of the Sutherlands and the Gedins was not misplaced. They had done their financial homework, and the figures did not add up. Gedin's statistics – which are no more than an extension of the statistics produced in Anthony Blond's earlier *The Publishing Game* – are an eloquent demonstration of the difficulties involved, in the 1970s, of publishing a novel by a serious writer and making money out of it.

Gedin and Sutherland's perspective on the state of fiction was broadly economic. But the uncertainty went deeper than that. For, as a book like *Fiction and the Fiction Industry* makes clear, the uncertainties which surrounded the production of fiction were reflected in the uncertainties surrounding its composition. One of Sutherland's exemplars – Kay Dick – went so far as to make an explicit connection: 'I . . . feel very pessimistic about things in general, particularly about things in England. No, I don't foresee a very agreeable future for any of us. I think it's very discouraging for a novelist that fewer and fewer books get read.' If it was a bad time economically, it was also a bad time creatively. If novelists had trouble getting their work published and the price of hardback fiction was prohibitively high, then it seemed axiomatic, at a time of generally impaired national morale, that the quality of the writing itself would suffer.

Equating broad political trends with the progress of a highly stylised artform is a facile business at the best of times. But the assumption of a deterioration in the novelist's standing and a deterioration in the work he or she produced is a characteristic of the wider fringes of literary journalism in the 1970s. Late in the decade, in what was to be almost its final issue, *The New Review* devoted most of a summer number to a symposium on 'The State of Fiction', drawing up a list of eighty prominent novelists and short-story writers and asking them two questions: How would they describe the development of fiction in English over the past ten years or so? And what developments did they hope for over the next decade? The replies are worth looking at even now as a résumé of what had gone before and a suggestion of what was to come. There are the usual wayside hilarities customarily associated with this sort of venture (the avant-garde lady novelist whose reply to question two is: 'an opening out, a taking off') but also the sober reflection of the Amises (senior and junior), Bradbury, Byatt, McEwan – people whose opinion on the state of fiction might be worth having.

Inevitably, at a decade's remove, most of the information is entirely trivial. There are references to books which are long-forgotten and earnest contributions by people few now have heard of. Who is there now, I wonder, who reads the novels of Mervyn Jones, or Helen Muir or Jeremy Brooks? There was also the ventilation of current controversy – Public Lending Right was a big issue at the time – the settling of ancient scores and the airing of some ferocious grudges. Several writers, more or less forgivably, use the forum as an excuse to complain that their books aren't in print or that no one will buy the American rights to their latest novel, written with the express purpose of knocking Henry James into a cocked hat. Elsewhere, however, the air is notably pessimistic. Amid the usual complaints about the corrosive influence of the mass media, Francis King strikes a note of elegant despair. There are no younger writers worth the name, reviews are asinine. There is a requirement for novelists to 'recover their status in the eyes of the public . . . to recover their nerve'. What has gone wrong? It is Sutherland's point all over again: it was precisely what had gone wrong with the economy. 'Not lack of inventiveness or lack of hard work or lack of ambition . . . but lack of confidence,' King claimed, and his conclusion has an authentic ring of silver-age declension: 'Of course novels will go on being written and, of course, from time to time a good or even a superb novelist will emerge. But soon the novelist will find, as the poet has found already, that the majority even of "educated" people have become totally uninterested in whatever freakish thing it is that he is trying to accomplish.'

King blames the public, a common enough resort of the disgruntled senior novelist even now. Other correspondents are charitable enough to assume that some of the blame might be ascribed to the writer. Kingsley Amis reveals: 'On the rare occasions when I dip into their work –' ('they' being a clutch of younger colleagues) '– I am struck by what looks at first like carelessness, malapropisms and other stylistic goofs, wooden dialogue, meagre characterisation. And I suppose it is that in a way – the carelessness of writers who aren't interested in language or literature or even people as individuals.' This, it might be fair to assume, is the characteristic 1970s complaint about standards given an exclusively artistic focus, and

Jennifer Johnson has a piteous line or two about the 'sheer bad craftsmanship' which 'makes you cringe as you read'. It begs several questions. Was there ever – a few mad lads excepted – a writer who wasn't interested in language? Or people – again excepting a handful of bug-eyed theorists? There is a way in which every age seems a little more philistine than the age which preceded it, at any rate to those it supplants.

Ah, the oldster lament for lost decencies! It is worth remembering that even the reviewers of 1917 thought Eliot a drunken helot. Yet the sense of there being some sort of stagnation in fiction, a loss of nerve, a technical accomplishment unsupported by ambition, is not confined to these fluent and unwearied pens. Mervyn Jones's summary reflects a common complaint: 'All over the place people are writing – usually in about six weeks – relatively accomplished but essentially trivial novels in which the reach is never felt to exceed the grasp.' Eva Figes thought that 'for me the old forms are hopelessly inadequate and can only say things that are no longer worth saying: we know all about them'. A young Ian McEwan, after a discussion of various fictional orthodoxies prevailing in the 1970s, concluded that: 'No one who is widely read is writing exploratory fiction interestingly critical of the world we live in. No one has developed any confident alternative to the dominant strain.' The artistic dead-end theory is one of the most convenient fictions of fiction, or at any rate of fiction writers – it can be used to explain away everything from laziness to sheer bad writing – but it pervades these accumulations of late 1970s writerly opinion, the brooding of embittered theorists and the laments of neglected reputations.

The New Review symposium is useful not so much for what it tells us about the state of English writing ten years ago – it was bad, but then we knew that already – but in what it tells us about writers' expectations of their art. This, I suppose, is the difference between the middlebrow crowd-pleaser and the highbrow 'serious novelist'. The one wants to ensure a decent standard of living for himself and his family;

the other – well, he just has expectations of his art. And as one might expect, these eighty or so analyses of the way in which fiction gets written are chock-full of assumptions of what the novel ought to do and about the writer's function. The key words turn up on every page: 'progress', 'development', 'experiment'. There is a widespread conviction that the novel ought to be 'exploratory', that there is some distant yet perceptible goal which each individual pen should be angled towards; there are frequent references to 'the world we live in' and 'society'. Inevitably, encouraging eighty people to sound off about the function of the novel results in a certain confusion. The effect of this avid colloquy is like watching a hundred cracker mottoes pass consecutively before your eyes: edified, initially, you end up stupefied by contradictory good sense. But some basic beliefs of the serious writer loom up at the reader like warning lights through fog. They might be summarised thus:

> *The novel has a purpose (though we are not sure what it is).*
> *The novel ought to 'progress' (though we are not sure in which direction).*
> *The novel is about 'the world we live in', though it has less and less relation to it.*
> *There is a mild conviction that serious writing ought to be in some way 'experimental' though we agree that any book labelled an 'experimental novel' is likely to be unreadable.*
> *None of us is likely to make any money out of the above.*

So much for the 1970s. I doubt that a similar collection of writers coralled together in the late 1980s would be as introspective, as downbeat or as downhearted. But the 1960s and 1970s had been a time at which much was expected of the novel and when – a symbiosis perhaps – novelists harboured an ambitious sense of what they might achieve. Eva Figes observes, with what now seems beguiling naivety: 'I was young enough to believe that eventually I and a few other writers with similar ideas would change the face of British writing.' What were Eva Figes's ideas? They (or ideas very like them) will be discussed in another chapter, but it is enough to say here that they didn't work and that nobody who mattered paid the slightest shred of attention to them. *The New Review*'s contributors are in no doubt that experimental fiction, whatever that was, had been tried and found wanting. But they were in no doubt either that the ordinary novel, the sort of book that gets discussed in the newspapers, that people buy or borrow from the libraries, was somehow failing to do its job; that a gap existed between fiction and the environment it attempted to describe.

Navel-gazing by writers can be uniquely tiresome. It is surely no longer necessary for anyone to explain that fiction is cognate with the verb 'to feign', that words are lies and that all, ultimately, is dissimulation and artifice. Still less is it necessary for the spikier sort of novelist to wonder publicly whether there is an 'about' for a novel to be about, or for the stiffer type to complain that novels aren't 'realistic' any more: after all, could anything be less realistic than our reality, when you pause to think about it? But the 1970s was a self-absorbed, self-referential decade. In some ways the pessimism of *The New Review* symposiasts was misplaced. The marginalisation of writers is not the clear-cut process that once it seemed. Television and the nastier aspects of the mass media have not quite displaced fiction in the manner that once seemed inevitable. In many ways books and their creators continue to fill a disproportionately large position in the public consciousness. In blunt terms, it is still possible to make a living out of it. Neither was the 1970s quite the Sahara of non-achievement that it is now sometimes made out to be. If it was the time of *The Glittering Prizes*, the telenovel and the outrageous hype, then it was also the time of *First Love, Last Rites*, of *Fireflies*, *Grimus* and *Dead Babies*. For the reader, making his own private treaties with a succession of writers of his choosing, these types of value judgement can seem inherently futile. The few expressions of optimism to emerge from *The New Review* look forward to an end to categories and compartments. A. S. Byatt hopes that more English novels will '. . . devise forms for subject matter that can't be categorised or labelled as "realistic" or "experimental" but will draw on whatever they need in an eclectic way'. Ominously, Paul Bailey suggests that 'with even more luck there will be no books at all about the State of the Novel'. As I say, it was a self-absorbed, self-referential decade. Bergonzi's *The Situation of the Novel*, John Gardner's *On Moral Fiction*, David Lodge's *The Novelist at the Crossroads*. The list of slightly anguished slabs of analysis would fill a decent-sized bookshelf. By the time *The New Review* came round to asking writers what they thought, one or two were entitled to feel that they were being got at.

Many of the names which turn up in *The New Review* assemblage would feature in any similar exercise conducted today: Kingsley Amis, Drabble, Storey, Murdoch, Wilson (Angus rather than A. N.). These are McEwan's 'dominant strain'. Fowles gets a mention here and there, and there are appreciative references to Spark and Bradbury. Youthful talent is represented by McEwan himself and Martin Amis. Rushdie, Mo and Carey have yet to come marching over the horizon and 'Commonwealth literature' is the preserve of V. S. Naipaul and Patrick White. Americans, brought in for the purposes of favourable comparison, include Barth, Pynchon, Doctorow and Vonnegut. Almost at once you are struck by an air of familiarity – at any rate on this side of the channel – and an absence of new faces. Amis and Murdoch have been on the bestseller lists for thirty-five years. Margaret Drabble wrote her first book in 1961. There is nothing intrinsically wrong in this, though there is perhaps something wrong with the length of the waiting list to join this pantheon. Critics impose long sentences of immaturity on young writers in Britain: Martin Amis has been writing fiction for upwards of fifteen years but still there is a suspicion of a callow youngster, a talent developing in minute hops and skips which will one day 'mature' and produce something 'significant'. It is sometimes possible to feel, casting a weather eye over British fiction and the prodigiously long careers it harbours, that a decade is too short a time, merely a brief stopping point on the trajectory of a writer's development.

Ah yes, development. Consult any periodical or textbook that professes to take literature seriously, watch one of those solemn Channel Four arts programmes in which men with beards discourse on books, and you can be fairly certain of finding someone cracking on about 'developments' in the novel, or better still 'movements' in British fiction. The notion that art should develop is a common one: in the 1970s it was even applied to pop music, with the result that a clutch of po-faced synthesiser players found themselves classified as 'progressive rock'. But it takes only a few moments' thought to explode this pedagogue's trick, this pundit's formulation. In fact, measured over the three hundred or so years of its existence, the English novel has scarcely developed at all. Comparing, say, *Vanity Fair* to Evelyn Waugh's *Sword of Honour* trilogy I cannot detect any development, I can only see two different novelists reacting to society in a way conditioned by their own social and psychological backgrounds. Even the stylistic trickery, the technical advances over which critics occasionally squawk, are seldom as newfangled as everyone supposes. It used to be customary, for instance, to refer to Ronald Firbank's novels, with their dislocated dialogue, their talking heads and their impression of conversational crosstalk, as technically innovative, but there is not a very great distance between them and some of the rustic chatter that characterises a Hardy novel like *Two on a Tower*, and the primal influence on Firbank goes back as far as Congreve.

This is not to say that novelists cannot find different and apparently superior ways of doing things. Going back to Firbank, his ability to contrive an atmosphere of menace by means of innocuous-sounding dialogue and the fragments of incidental plot strewn through the text strike me as more or less original, but they are minor, wayside felicities. Part of Firbank's charm is that he is sending up, burlesquing an existing tradition, rather than constructing a new one. Much the same could be said of Joyce, who is perhaps more interesting and powerful as a writer when he is subverting staid conventions than manufacturing the dream language of *Finnegan's Wake*. While you can forgive the critics who refer to fiction as 'organic', it is a mistake to regard the novel as some rapidly evolving animal, continually sprouting new limbs of awareness, perception and technique, or as a juggernaut racing towards some distant goal of explanation or elucidation. Clever people will always write books about what is known as 'the human condition' and that is about all there is to it. Generally speaking, the more self-conscious the attempt at experiment, the more resounding the call (remember Eva Figes with her attempt to 'change the face of British fiction'), the more certain is the likelihood of failure. Even twenty years ago, when experimental writing was all the rage and the contents of a new B. S. Johnson novel were offered to its purchasers in a cardboard box – there was an earlier one, I seem to remember, which had holes cut in it to allow the reader to see the ending while reading the beginning; a sort of fast-forward effect – everyone was glumly conscious that another attempt at innovation had fallen flat on its face.

But if it is absurd to expect novelists to 'develop' in any meaningful sense of the word, it is not too much to expect them to change. This is almost too elementary a formulation to be worth stating. Society changes, people change, books ought to change as well – in theme, if not in technique. One feature of the last twenty years has been the concern with the fringes of the Women's Movement, reflected not so much in subject matter – though there have been plenty of books about confident *Cosmo* girls highstepping it from one bumper orgasm to the next – as in an examination of the women's point of view on a whole range of issues. Again, this is not quite as newfangled as it sounds – plenty of Victorian men wrote lucid examinations of the woman's point of view – but it could be argued a novel like Ian McEwan's *The Comfort of Strangers*, a scary dissection of sexual politics, could not have been written before the late 1970s.

Naturally enough, this argument only holds good if you accept the conventional nostrum of what the novel does. For years people have talked pompously about the 'Function of the Novel'. (What am I doing now? That's right, I'm talking pompously about the function of the novel.) It has led to tiny, unassuming rectangles of prose being seen as Marxist building blocks or guidebooks for life. Lately, what with the 'Death of the Author' and the rest of the post-structuralist package, it has led to writers and their work sinking beneath a tide of theory which concerns itself with decoding and textual transmission, which insists that the words rather than the people who assemble them are important. It is easy to mock the theorists, to snigger at the whirl of intellectual skywriting taking place far above our heads, to marvel at its self-absorption and its consistent lack of interest in the concerns of the ordinary writer and reader, but it is also easy to forget the genuine contribution which structuralism – itself a ragbag of other 'isms' – has made to criticism. The point of a text is often what is absent from it. Taking a book to pieces, unravelling its signs, structures and themes, can often radically alter our perceptions of a novel. The drawback, as every writer who has ever interested himself in theory will admit, is that modern notions of *intertextualité* and the 'transmission of the text' bear no relation to the actual processes of literary composition. It is the difference between an architect drawing up a groundplan and the labourer tugging lumps of concrete around a muddy field. Unsurprisingly, no one – no ordinary reader – can ever look at a modern work of literary criticism without occasionally resenting the remoteness of the attitudes displayed within it. Patently the reader who imagines that *Little Dorrit* is a novel about a little girl in a Victorian debtor's prison and the critic who thinks it is a sort of metaphor for thermodynamics (I am not exaggerating – an American called

George Levine did this recently in an essay entitled '*Little Dorrit* and three kinds of science') are hardly reading the same book.

In any case, theory proceeds with wilful disregard for what it is that the novelist does and what it is that the reader expects from him: the reason why all the 'experimental' novels of the 1960s and 1970s, the books written with one eye on Barthes and the Yale critical school, sank without trace is that they were inferior pieces of writing and there was no pleasure to be gained from reading them. This chasm between what the reader wants to read and what the criticial sophisticate thinks that he ought to read is another example of the fragmentation of literary culture, and it obscures the fact that, essentially, the decent novelist does very few things: he or she entertains, conveys what Martin Amis once called the 'staid satisfactions' of plot, pace and narrative, and acts consciously or unconsciously as a social registrar. Every first-rate book does this, those by novelists who deliberately masquerade as social historians, those by novelists who are more interested in unravelling their own psychology, stitch by stitch on to the page. In this respect there is no particular difference between, say, *The Way We Live Now* and *The Trial*. Trollope's novel is a scrupulous piece of mid-Victorian realism, an anatomy of a society sinking into a slough of venal commercialism; Kafka's is a grim *mitteleuropa* allegory of paranoia, but they are both 'interestingly critical', to use McEwan's phrase, of the society which produced them. Moreover, anyone who likes to talk about Kafka's 'development' should examine Trollope's psychological symbolism. Increasingly, looking at the 'realist' masterpieces of the Victorian age you are led to the conclusion that there is no such thing as realism.

But then categorisation makes fools of us all. Talk to the reader of modern English fiction about 'development', 'progress' and 'experiment', even talk to him about books being 'interestingly critical' and he will call you a fool. Where does all this shuffling of packs of cards marked 'reality', 'illusion' and 'artifice' leave the English novel at the end of the 1980s? First, it is of course an unquestionable fact that the English don't read serious books. They never have done, and critics have been complaining about it since the 1570s when Thomas Nashe protested that 'copies of *Tom Thumbe*' stood piled up on the booksellers' tables while better work lay dead. It is not even true to say, as people occasionally say of the Victorians, that 'well, Dickens was popular': Mrs Leavis's researches proved that he was outsold by the penny dreadfuls, mid-Victorian *schlock* like *Varney the Vampire* and *Maria Monk*, by a factor of approximately five to one. But at least Dickens was a public figure. To the mass of 'educated' people today Martin Amis, McEwan and Ackroyd are no more than names. Yet despite this general neglect there is each year a tiny, tiny season in which 'serious novels' are widely discussed and commented on: the season of literary prizes, notably the Booker and the Whitbread, leading up to the Christmas run-in when publishers start unloading yet more of their wares on to an already glutted market.

Amid the fuss which greets a Booker winner, which will produce sales of 30–40,000 copies and see all the author's other books which nobody bought dusted down and put on the shelves again, it is important to view the British fiction industry in context. Something over 6,000 new novels get published every year, nearly half of them in the autumn when publishers' lists grow steadily more cluttered and the books pages of the national newspapers begin to resemble one of those expanding suitcases into which you can always cram another couple of items. Perhaps a fifth of them have some pretensions to respectability – that is to say they are 'literary' novels which will attract half-a-dozen reviews, sell about 1,000 copies, and, if everybody is very lucky, go into paperback.

What are they like, these books which don't sell but are for the most part so compliantly received by their critics? To read most book reviewers you would think that we luxuriate in a sort of Golden Age of English fiction, a world of promising literary youngsters, maturing middle-aged talents, sage elders casting a benign eye on the hotbed of experiment and innovation that seethes below them. We don't. A look at last year's Booker shortlist – Rushdie, Carey, Fitzgerald, Chatwin, Warner and Lodge – bereft of youthful talent, its two heavyweight writers respectively Indian and Australian, confirms this. We live at a time when the relationship between the novel of ideas and the (usually comic) novel of action, between drawing-room twitter and the banana skin, has become ever more distant. We live at a time when the 'literary novel', for so long a more or less accurate reflection of the way in which people thought and felt, has become a stylised abstraction, a time when English writers have lost whatever glamour they once possessed. It is no use going around pretending that contemporary writing in this country is frightfully good. It is, in fact, frightfully bad.

It takes scant analysis to establish the wretched standing of most domestic writing. Where is the English novelist below the age of thirty-five of whom it can be predicted that he or she will in some way, however marginally, change the face of the novel? This is a risky prediction, perhaps, but half a century ago it could confidently have been made of Waugh, Powell, Greene and Isherwood. Where, for that matter, is the British writer with the international status of a García Márquez, a Vidal, a Grass or a Kundera? Observers on this side of the channel may gnash their teeth over Kundera's influence and what are seen as his highbrow posturings – it was interesting to note that the recent cinema version of *The Unbearable Lightness of Being* attracted all the usual highbrow-baiting epithets – but the fact remains that he *matters* in any discussion of European high culture, in a way in which English writers do not. Only Golding perhaps, a maverick who stands a little way outside the English tradition, and Iris Murdoch, a writer customarily viewed as a philosopher *manquée*, have any sort of international presence.

Inevitably this sort of comparison is unfair. It takes a very special mixture of social and political circumstance to produce a Kundera or a García Márquez, and it presupposes a literary tradition which this country has never been able or rarely even wanted to assimilate. To a degree it is unfair to mention English writers in the context of a culture which most would ignore and not a few entirely repudiate. After all, 'European high culture' is a phrase which would have your average critic – an Auberon Waugh, an A. N. Wilson – reaching for a metaphorical shotgun. But if one could accuse senior English novelists of insularity, of lacking any sort of coherent worldview – and it has never been the case that to possess a 'worldview' was a criterion of literary ability – one could not accuse them of lacking ambition. The late 1980s have been remarkable for the pack of books unleashed upon us by the old guard of English letters, writers with long-term views on what has happened to us all in the years since the war: Kingsley Amis, Frederic Raphael, Margaret Drabble, John Wain. They are all still with us, these people, all intending to stick around for *a very long time*, all writing novels whose aims have been to sum up a decade or an era. They have ambitious titles (Raphael's *After the War*) and ambitious aims: Drabble's *The Radiant Way*, for instance, was widely publicised as a real state-of-the-nation book, 'a powerful novel for the 1980s'. They are, without exception, bad books. It is difficult to convey in a few sentences just how poor a novel is Kingsley Amis's *Difficulties with Girls*, for example, how unfunny, how bereft of any relation to its time, how its analysis of a milieu – the 1960s – is not much more than a roster of bigotry.

It is facile to accuse a novelist of 'failing': it is usually a task performed by people without the slightest inclination or ability to write fiction themselves. The axiom about those who can doing and those who can't teaching is at least as applicable to literature as to any other area of human activity. On one level *War and Peace* is a failure. Amis, Drabble and the others fail because they are unable to perceive, or do not wish to, the powerful forces at work in society which really influence the way in which we think and act: America, television, the global money marketplace, and especially language, the constantly revivifying, endlessly self-renewing language of transatlantic and transcontinental culture. Language. There are several complaints which it is possible to level at the domestic senior common-room: a terrible uncertainty in the realm of ideas, a wilful disregard of social change, but chief among them is linguistic niggardliness. Understandably, this is a thought that seems to occur more regularly to American critics. Here is John Updike, from an essay that appeared in the collection *Hugging the Shore*: 'It is a rare sentence of his prose that surrenders to the demon of language, that abdicates a seat of fussy social judgement, that is there for its own sake, out of simple awe, gratitude or dismay in the face of creation.' He is talking about Kingsley Amis, but the words could apply to half-a-dozen of our 'senior novelists', the generation of post-war writers who abdicated their responsibilities and left as a legacy a shelf of feeble contemporary novels, who assumed that you could go on endlessly writing the same type of book in the same type of voice, and that everything, transfixed and immutable, would go on as before.

There are several quite complicated long-term explanations for novelists' inability to write meaningful books about the society they inhabit. One is that this society has grown too complex, its gradations at once too random and too subtle for writers to undertake the great, satisfying analyses of the past. It is impossible to write a novel like *Middlemarch* in the last decade of the 20th century, however much Melvyn Bragg or Margaret Drabble may think otherwise. Equally, it is impossible to resist the conclusion that they and a tribe of lesser writers are labouring vainly to write the sort of book that can no longer be written. Most of our 'great writers', these mastodons of modern English literature, are simply not capable of defining the 1980s. Whenever an accomplished and specifically English novelist does emerge – a Peter Ackroyd, say, or a Graham Swift – it is significant that he moves *backwards*. *Hawksmoor* and *Waterland* were brilliant books, and their brilliance lay in that they used the past, and in Ackroyd's case the language of the past, to reinterpret the present. The half-tone, the oblique angle. Confronted with bleak unpromising reality the English novelist seldom ripostes, but he is usually able to *deflect*. These are some of the reasons perhaps why, internationally, English fiction is little more than a joke and why the English novel, that venerable and resourceful institution, is invariably seen as something factitious, something artifically kept alive, like the Old Time Music Hall or the Punch and Judy show.

Writing about writing has its own built-in inconsistencies. No survey of any department of literature is anything other than selective and, by implication, misrepresentative. The most compulsive enthusiast, even if he devoted most of his spare time to modern literary fiction, would only get through a fifth of the annual output. The most diligent book reviewer – someone who is a top-notcher in his profession and makes a fair proportion of his living out of criticism – might see a hundred. Moreover, there is a reasonable chance that he is not even seeing the 'right' books. Most critics only get sent the stuff from the big publishing houses: the small press working from somebody's kitchen table, the amateur who decides to publish at his own expense, even paperback originals, are characteristically ignored. There is a strong strain of vivid domestic writing produced outside London, confined to regional arts magazines and limited edition pamphlets, which is never taken up by commercial publishers.

Separating books into these watertight compartments is one drawback. Another is the long tradition of attacks on an art form which has proved surprisingly resilient to critics who locate in it evidence of terminal malaise. There has seldom been a group of literary critics who did not in some way assume the decadence of the books on which they were asked to comment. The whey-faced scribblers, the superannuated poets and dingy hacks who populate Gissing's *New Grub Street* are in no doubt that most contemporary novels are sheer trash. This type of attitude is very common, so much so that one scarcely raises an eyebrow at *The New Review* symposiast who opened his contribution: 'In a decadent society – that it is, agreement would be fairly general – weeds flourish, exotic and abundant.' One of the most enduring intellectual habits is to assume that everything is very bad and can only get worse. Consequently, nearly every decade produces some 'defence' of the novel which, typically, opens with a statement of the opposing case:

It hardly needs pointing out that at this moment the prestige of the novel is extremely low, so low that the words 'I never read novels', which even a decade ago were generally uttered with a hint of apology, are now *always* uttered in a tone of conscious pride. It is true that there are still a few contemporary or roughly contemporary novelists whom the intelligentsia consider it permissible to read; but the point is that the ordinary good-bad novel is habitually ignored while the ordinary good-bad book of verse or criticism is still taken seriously . . . Even now the novel is visibly deteriorating, and it would deteriorate much faster if most novelists had any idea who reads their books. It is, of course, easy to argue (*vide* for instance Belloc's queerly rancorous essay) that the novel is a contemptible form of art and that its fate does not matter. I doubt whether that opinion is even worth disputing. At any rate, I am taking it for granted that the novel is worth salvaging and that in order to salvage it you have got to persuade intelligent people to take it seriously. It is therefore worthwhile to analyse one of the main causes – in my opinion, *the* main cause – of the novel's lapse in prestige.

Orwell – for it is he – is writing in 1936 (interestingly, he adduces the main cause of the novel's lapse in prestige as ineffectual reviewers). At the time this was a fair reaction to a great deal of contemporary cant, the *Sunday Times* reviewers who could inform their readers that 'if you can read this book and not scream with delight, then your soul is dead'. But if it was the age of Walpole and Ralph Straus and the public ecstasies over Priestley, then it was also the age of *Love on the Dole*, *A Handful of Dust*, and, to give Orwell his occasionally neglected due, *Burmese Days*. Anthony Powell had written *Venusberg*, Isherwood had begun work on *Mr Norris*. If this was a cultural desert, then various oases lay close at hand. Moreover, Orwell's analysis of his own age and its shortcomings makes a useful yardstick by which to compare our own. Looking at some of the novels he was required to pronounce on in the *New English Weekly* ('After this we take a dive into the sewers of literature' are his opening remarks on one of them) it is hard not to feel that the general standard of writing has rather improved, that the number of people who can hold a pen has radically increased. Whether anyone reads them or has any particular interest in what they say is another matter.

Sooner or later anyone who devotes large amounts of his time to reading and writing about fiction will find himself having to answer three basic questions: First, what is a 'good' novel? Second, what are my credentials for attempting to make such a definition? Third, does any of it matter? (There is a fourth, related, question about the usefulness of criticism, but most book reviewers value their self-respect too highly to formulate it.) The answers – and I imagine they apply to anyone who has ever ventured into print with 'This week's fiction round-up' – are these:

1. There is no definition of a 'good' novel. There are novels which are plausible and novels which are implausible. In fact, any attempt at definition is likely to be unhelpful. Like the pupils of Dotheboys Hall we know that a horse is a gramnivorous quadruped but we are not sure that this tells you anything revealing about a horse. Each of us has inside his head a scale of literary values capable of accommodating an infinite number of half-tones. *Scarlet and Black* is a 'good'

novel and so is Priestley's *Angel Pavement* and so – up to a point – is the latest George Macdonald Fraser, but to construct a critical approach capable of containing them all, short of a structuralist sign system, would be to sacrifice all for the casual generalisation. The reader works by instinct, even if he is not always entirely sure what that instinct is.

2. My credentials are, inevitably, those of the typical white, male, middle-class reader. Fiction began for me at the age of three with the *Tales of Beatrix Potter*, continued with dramatisations of the life of 15th-century pageboys, read aloud by prep school mistresses, and reached some sort of pubertal apogee with *The Lord of the Rings*, which at thirteen seemed to me the finest book that anyone, anywhere, had ever written or could write. My only complaint was that it was not half as long again. Then came Orwell. It is impossible to convey in words the effect that a novel like *Keep the Aspidistra Flying* has on a bookish, factitiously disaffected schoolboy. 'He knows all about me', you feel, 'he wrote this specially for me' (which is what Orwell said about Henry Miller). The pose of bookish disaffection is a seductive one. At school I was the child who sits at the back of the classroom cradling a copy of *Lord of the Flies* behind the cover of *Elementary Physics volume one* and wondering which tyrannical deity has ordained this monotonous thraldom, the child who bunks off games in favour of the set of Anthony Powell novels in the school library. A little later there was 'A' level English literature, during the course of which somebody suggested that I was 'reasonably well-read for a boy of his age'. That did it. I spent quite a lot of time finding out about English literature. To be precise I spent an entire summer holidays finding out about English literature. I found out about English literature at the rate of twenty books a week. Monday: *Hard Times, Vile Bodies, Under the Greenwood Tree*. Tuesday: *The History of Mr Polly, Roderick Random* . . . A little later in the time off between school and university, when you were supposed to be travelling the world or undergoing similar

fatuities, there was the friendly bookshop where I alternated between keeping an eye on the stock and reading it. A little later still there was university where Professor Trevor-Roper's lectures were of rather less interest than the bound volumes of Thackeray in the college library. Thackeray. Trollope. Gissing. Dreiser. London. Joyce. James T. Farrell. Styron . . . Why read fiction? At heart I suppose – this applies whether the author is Proust or Catherine Cookson, and knocks away most of the arguments advanced in this book – you read fiction to escape, to bring into your own life the rewarding tensions that would otherwise be absent from it. Books, it scarcely needs saying, are life lived at one remove. I feel about novels the way I felt at twelve about association football, the way I felt at eighteen about rock and roll. At bottom the critic is nothing more than a fan – or a performer *manqué*.

3. Literature, in that it is primarily a personal, solipsistic pleasure, typically has large claims made for it, claims which are very much resented. Writers who compose letters to the newspapers or choose to comment on anything other than the business of writing are commonly harried by the right-wing press for betraying evidence of 'self-importance'. One of the truly depressing things about the Salman Rushdie affair was the number of times it found some pop-eyed columnist hoping that the result wouldn't be to make writers feel 'uppish'. Of course, in one very obvious way books are not important. A novel is less important than a roof over your head and a good deal less important than a square meal. Most people, I suspect, would cheerfully consign the complete collected works of D. H. Lawrence to oblivion if it meant that some aspect of human suffering might be alleviated. These are false distinctions, but sometimes listening to the art-and-beauty school of literary criticism you feel compelled to make them. And books *do* matter. Like Orwell, I take it for granted that the serious novel has an important function and that it is something intelligent people ought to read. Perhaps the most favourable consequence of the row over *The Satanic Verses* – and one

had to search hard to find any – was its demonstration that the book can still exist as a weapon. In the age of political Ayatollahs and the SS-20, in the age of corporate rather than individual thought, in the age – to move a little nearer home – of satellite television, the *Daily Mail* and Mr Peregrine Worsthorne, that is not perhaps a bad thing.

II

Writers, Politics and Society

Today writers are constantly urged towards commitment, which usually means direct identification with some prevailing ideological system . . . Such systems are often the selfish, vulgate myths . . . of sectors in the society who, seeing the historical process as the only thing that matters, seek in the long or short run to monopolise it.

Malcolm Bradbury,
The Social Context of Modern English Literature

Different countries treat their writers in different ways. In Peru the novelist Mario Vargas Llosa was asked to stand for the presidency in 1990. In America novelists can run for the Senate, stage fiery disputations with White House apologists or swear that they 'won the election for Kennedy'. In Nicaragua a bunch of guerrilla poets ended up by forming a government. Sartre hung out on the barricades. Imagining the British equivalent of these high-profile engagements takes one off into flights of lurid fantasy. Martin Amis fights a by-election on a No Nukes, End to American Bases ticket. A. N. Wilson pilots his controversial bill on church disestablishment through a packed House of Commons. Julian Barnes, as leader of an impoverished inner-city council, gets surcharged for disregarding government-imposed spending limits and goes on a 'terminal' hunger strike. In many ways this does not only seem implausible but undesirable. The writer as political activist, whose motives are no less confused and devious than those of anyone else, generally ends up by making a terrific fool of himself. By all accounts Mailer on the campaign trail for the mayorality of New York (where he came next to nowhere) was a deeply embarrassing spectacle; and we all know what happened to Mishima.

But though an air of genteel quietism has hung lazily over the English novel, manifesting itself occasionally in the conviction that art is somehow 'above' politics or that no civilised person would ever want to bother himself with the governance of his country, there is a long and fairly honourable tradition of writers intervening or interfering in domestic politics. Naturally, this is not something that officialdom has ever welcomed. Characteristically the relationship between writers and politicians has always been uneasy, a fragile dialogue liable to distortion, resentment and cheerful malice. It is said that Macaulay declined to review *Hard Times* on account of its 'sullen socialism', and how much socialism is there in *Hard Times*? But then it used to be customary to refer to Cubist paintings as 'Bolshevist', and even today, in the wake of countless revisionist biographies, it is never quite possible to rid Kipling of the tag 'Imperialist writer'.

That this sort of resentment persists is a testimony to the compartmentalisation of modern life. Even today the notion that a novelist might have political ideas floating about in his head and might want to give them a public airing is calculated to make the average newspaper columnist seethe with rage. The 1987 General Election campaign was remarkable for the ardour with which right-wing papers attacked various writers, dramatists and whatnot who had made the indelicate mistake of announcing that they intended to vote Labour. In this atmosphere of suspicion it is hardly surprising that the most recent engagement between the pen and the Statute Book, Lady Antonia Fraser's little dinner for a group of anti-Thatcherite writers and the establishment of the June 20 group, quickly declined into a riot of personal attacks. What did Lady Antonia think she knew about it? What, for that matter, did any pen pusher think that he or she knew about anything? It is a queer paradox, this. Journalists on all sides cry out for writers to be 'relevant' and as soon as they perform an act as relevant as expressing a political preference they are somehow seen to be engaged in a sort of spiritual trespassing.

Yet the gathering *au côté de chez Fraser* did at least ventilate the comparatively musty issue of writers and political commitment, the question of what a writer thinks about the way in which society is controlled and administered. This resolves itself into a number of broad questions; not so much: why should a writer bother to have political opinions and presume to prosecute them? (not even a Conservative backbencher could swallow that one) but: is it possible, amid the dense and unpromising chaos that surrounds us, for writers to influence people? If so, how? If not, why not? On the face of it nothing could be more straightforward. X the novelist writes a book read by reader Y who, after mature reflection, allows it to colour his views as to matter Z. This ignores the fact that no art is simply message, but admits the power of novels to effect change. When Upton Sinclair wrote *The Jungle*, his famous exposé of the turn-of-the-century Chicago meat-packing factories, there was a public outcry and the laws were changed within months. You can just imagine the bureaucratic recrimination, the legal rearguard actions, the closing of ranks on the part of vested interests that would spring neatly into place if, for instance, someone were to write a novel set in a Suffolk village about the carcinogenic effects of the local power station. In 1904 the mechanisms which linked art and society were substantially more clear-cut.

In any case, all this leaves aside a much more vital and intrinsic question. What is a 'political' text? Well, *Lysistrata* is. And so is Trollope's *The Prime Minister*, and Robert Tressell's *The Ragged Trousered Philanthropists* and Kafka's *The Castle* (Greek drama, drawing-room novel, Edwardian polemic, modernist allegory – they are all 'political' books). One could go further – it is not a particularly original progression – and say that all writing above the level of an instruction leaflet on a household appliance betrays, consciously or unconsciously, some form of political bias. Anyone who doubts this statement should look at a Women's Library of Love novelette and note the wide-eyed assumptions about sex and society which it cheerfully conveys. Curiously enough, telling a woman that it is the summit of human achievement to marry a bank manager and be able to afford a house with two bathrooms is a political statement. Obviously all art is propaganda, more or less. This is not to say that every novel is a political tract – in fact the more it resembles a political tract the less likely it is to be a good novel – but it does mean that every novel, even a spinster's demure analysis of everyday life in a country town, is capable of being decoded to reveal some of the assumptions on which society is based, the attitudes which underlie it and the forces which operate within it. This is as much true of a work of self-proclaimed 'realism' as of a piece of fantasy, the 'sheer escapism' customarily seen as an antidote to unwelcome reality. The Shire in *The Lord of the Rings* may be populated by small furry animals and visited by itinerant wizards but it is noticeable that the Hobbits arrange their lives in much the same way as the inhabitants of an early 20th-century English village, and there is a strong notion of the concept of deference.

For some reason the art-equals-politics equation has always scared people to death, people who fail to realise that 'art for art's sake' is still a political attitude (for a start, it is one of those attitudes that needs quite a lot of money to sustain it). Yet 'politics' at its simplest level means no more than 'the way society works'. *Middlemarch*, set at the time of the 1832 Reform Bill, is a political novel, but so is R. F. Delderfield's *God is an Englishman*, if only on the strength of its title, and so is the latest Catherine Cookson. Whether we like it or not, ideology and aesthetics are inseparable. Or rather not inseparable. In fact, they are the same thing.

It is strange that one has to labour this point, but we live at a time when there is no very great agreement as to what a book ought to do, or whether it ought to do anything at all. The art-for-art's-sake lobbyist, who still exists here and there like a fly trapped in amber, will tell you that the real world is simply not worth considering. The literary theorist will inform you that the significations imposed on life by fiction are arbitrary and therefore valueless. The post-modernist will explain – and the post-modernist has got a point – that the world has grown too complex, too *discombombulated*, for the leisured expositions of a Dickens or a Trollope. Given this confusion of motive, it is odd to have to defend a writer's political commitment, to point out that the novel is essentially a subversive art form, and that the mark of any decent novelist has always been a 'robust discontent' (the phrase belongs not to some fuzzy-haired Marxist but to Evelyn Waugh) with the conditions under which he or she laboured. But our expectations of writing in this country are desperately low. It is impossible, for instance, to read the review pages of a Sunday newspaper or one of the more right-wing weeklies without being struck by their languid air of complacency, their assumption that books should consist of Hampstead twitter, gentle mockery, 'fine writing' – all the qualities that lend modern English novels their shabby gloze.

For writers in this country commitment has nearly always been a crankish and hugely embarrassing affair, something callow, furtive and unsuccessful. In the 19th century novelists stood for parliament, their success in inverse proportion to their merit: Disraeli got in, Thackeray and Trollope didn't. (Trollope bequeathed a bitter memento in the electioneering episodes of *Ralph the Heir* which suggests that compared to the Victorians our own parliamentary system is not quite the swindle that we sometimes like to think it.) Osbert Sitwell tried to perform a backstairs role in the resolution of the 1926 General Strike, subsequently joined Mosley's New Party, and got out only just in time. Today, asked to name a novelist in whom punditry and some form of artistic purpose are combined most people would come up with a name like Kingsley Amis, a joke figure of the right. Peer leftward in search of something called 'socialist fiction', the sort of thing that Arthur Calder-Marshall used to write in the 1930s, and there is only a hole in the air. Certainly during the 1960s and 1970s there were writers who might be described as 'socialist novelists' – Mervyn Jones or the late Verity Bargate – but what little reputation they might have had is already dead.

Unquestionably the absence of any corpus of post-war English writing that could be labelled 'socialist literature' is linked to the failure to develop an authentic working-class literature in this country. It is worth turning aside for a moment to examine the question of the working-class writer – most of the literature of protest is inherently bourgeois – and asking why the social realism that affected the novel of the 1950s and 1960s, the 'angry young men' and their successors, did not become socialist realism. Orwell remarks somewhere in the course of a radio discussion on 'The Proletarian Writer' that there is no such thing as a working-class novelist because any working-class person who picks up a pen will inevitably write in a 'bourgeois' manner. At the time when Orwell was writing, such a statement – that for a working man to write a book was *in itself* a subtle act of emasculation – was not unreasonable. Neither was his contention that working-class writing scarcely existed. Look at the 'proletarian literature' of the first half of this century and what do you find? Tressell. Walter Greenwood's *Love on the Dole*, Jack Common and wads of 1930s Marxist fiction by superannuated public schoolboys. Applied to the literary scene of the 1950s and the type of novel that was supposed to reflect the point of view of the mythical working man, Orwell's argument is even neater. Not only were John Braine, Stan Barstow and the other Northern social realists writing in this bourgeois way, using bourgeois values, but their very aspirations were bourgeois. Their gutsy protagonists wanted houses and cars and a chunk of Macmillan's affluent society. Only in Sillitoe's Arthur Seaton do you find the sort of an-archic, purposeless vitality that somehow places the character outside the normal channels of ambition and achievement.

But Sillitoe's is not the only authentic working-class voice of this period. Sid Chaplin's novels, for instance, are not much read these days but their relation to this group of late 1950s writers is a significant one. While Chaplin's early books had a profound influence on Barstow, Sillitoe and Co. he did not produce his best work until the early 1960s, with the result that novels such as *The Day of the Sardine* and *The Watcher and the Watched* did not appear until much of the interest in this new Northern realism had subsided. Their keynote is authenticity, an immersion in the details of ordinary life that is quite unforced and matter-of-fact. Though Chaplin ended his working career as the National Coal Board's specialist writer he began it down the mine, and it was this perspective, more than any other, which coloured what he wrote. Most of Chaplin's strengths as a writer – and they are considerable – are displayed in *The Day of the Sardine*, published in 1961. In many ways it is a similar work to *Saturday Night and Sunday Morning* with Arthur Haggerston, its moody Tyneside hero, experiencing the same problems of older women and useless labour, the sense of being part of some imperfectly perceived system against which rebellion will always be futile. There is still aspiration, but it exists only as something to be mocked. 'Ah'm going to be somebody,' Arthur declaims ironically, '. . . get filthy rich, hob with the nobs, drive a Jaguar, have a private swimming pool.' It is a telling note. One of John Braine's heroes, you feel, might have said this and actually meant it.

Outlook apart, Chaplin's distinguishing feature is not his subject matter but his style: stark, elliptical blocks of sentences stripped of pronouns and prepositions. 'Once mentioned this . . . Times you want to scream.' It conveys the turns and cadences of local speech, but without mimicking the bourgeois manner which Orwell deprecated, and frequently rises to an odd, quirky lyricism. About the nearest thing to it in modern writing is James Kelman's evocation of life in urban Scotland: sharp fragments of prose that have a strangely voluptuous quality. Inevitably, though, you emerge from a book like *In Blackberry Time*, a collection of pieces which appeared shortly after Chaplin's death in 1986, with an impression only of remoteness, a sensation akin to staring at a cloche hat or a jar of hundreds-and-thousands. It is not simply that the world it descries is dead: a world of tightly-knit communities – the sort of world in which the whole street will gang up on the tallyman – organised labour and class solidarity. It is rather that Chaplin himself is a type of writer who has almost completely disappeared: one of those splendid Northern auto-didacts whose novels are on one level a conscious extension of their own lives. His young modern equivalent would be off to Oxford and a job at the BBC – a fine thing for him no doubt, but a career unlikely to inspire a book like *The Day of the Sardine*, which is in its way a better novel than many of the alleged landmarks of post-war British fiction.

In any case, neither Chaplin nor any of his contemporaries was in any way a political figure. There are obvious reasons why England since the war has not been an environment calculated to produce any examples of the novelist as poli-tician. At present to detect any sign of overt political involve-ment, involvement which works in that it annoys the power at which it is aimed, you have to look abroad, to J. M. Coetzee and Christopher Hope in South Africa (and before them Breytenbach), to Joseph Brodsky, to the samizdat writers of the East where, typically, political circumstance has tended to dictate specific and unusual styles. A dense and subtle satire like Iskander's *Sandro of Chegem*, which contains, *inter alia*, a stunning denunciation of Stalin's policy of collectivisation, is written with an exact conception of what the author can or cannot get away with. Similarly, the books which have marched out of Central and South America in the past twenty years, the tide of literature which Western taxonomy has marked down as 'magic realism', are in their way created by political circumstance. One might think that the corral erected around what is a heterodox group of writers is crazily artificial, but it acknowledges what separates them from much Anglo-Saxon writing: the ledger accounts of novels that try to be 'realistic' cannot accommodate the fractured landscapes of a

García Márquez or a Vargas Llosa. Thus García Márquez's most recent novel, *Love in the Time of Cholera*, is a set in a fragile Central American republic, whose rulers are always at war, whose inhabitants are always dying of disease and whose people are barely in control of their own lives. Such a world, García Márquez implies, lacks the staid axes and parameters we associate with representational fiction. If you live in a country whose contending factions have been at war for the last fifty years, where the immediate past is simply manufactured and there is a gleeful disregard for objective truth, then the chances are that sooner or later there will emerge a novel like *One Hundred Years of Solitude*, which created its own context and fashioned its own truths and contingencies out of myth. For the inhabitants of García Márquez's Central America there is no such thing as 'ordinary' chronology, there is only the present and the myths and symbols of a reinvented past.

Examining the achievements of the South Americans, or the international stature of the Solzhenitzyns and the Voinoviches, it would be fatally easy to assume that political involvement is born of necessity, that it is only in soft Western democracies that writers slumber gamely on, stretching a hand across the coverlet every so often to sign an Amnesty International petition in favour of someone they have never read, cranked into consciousness now and again to lobby against library cutbacks. A glance across the Atlantic quickly disproves this theory. After all, America was where Gore Vidal ran for Congress (he lost, but he got more votes than John Kennedy) and where Norman Mailer could stand for mayor of New York City, an interesting campaign in which the candidate proposed some 'existential legislation' which involved, among other things, death by gladiatorial combat for convicted murderers. To read the accounts of Vidal's annual state of the union address, a mocking parody of the presidential résumé ('I usually start with a prayer but instead I'll start with the latest Nancy Reagan joke' – there is a good description in Martin Amis's *The Moronic Inferno*) is to be split between an awareness that the whole thing is merely a vehicle for Vidal's paralysing cleverness and an acknowledgement that here is a writer, Christ, a *writer*, actually mixing it with corporate orthodoxy.

Of course, not every Western democracy wants or even needs the assistance of these self-engrossed publicists. Vidal and Mailer are at least as much showmen as politicians (but then so was Ronald Reagan). There is also the drawback that no right-minded person could even begin to take Mailer seriously. Yet matched against these monstrous, brooding presences, the British writer looks puny, out-of-focus. Americans stand sideways on to the whole intimate United States publicity machine which turns the successful writer into a guru, a literary god with rapt, unquestioning worshippers, something like Roth's alter ego in *Zuckerman Unbound*. As somebody once pointed out, if success comes to an American writer it changes his life. If it comes to a British writer – success being defined as winning the Booker Prize or getting a good American deal – he might nervously give up his job or buy a new filing cabinet. Naturally, it in no way increases the self-esteem of the British writer if you point this out to him. Esmé Lightfoot, let us say, author of *Advance*, *On the Margins* and *Subsidiary Rights* ('A first novel of deft accomplishment' – *Times Literary Supplement*) lurking around the fringes of international writers' conferences, darkly envious of the gentlemen from behind the Iron Curtain, does not want to be told that he is unread and unregarded. It is something of which he will already be keenly aware.

It is also something which, if the British writer has any sense of literary history, he will see as representing an obvious falling off, a retreat from a time when writers did not always fill this marginal, left-field position. Fifty years ago a certain type of English author basked in a sort of golden age of public interest and political fervour. It was the time of Gollancz's Left Book Club, of cultural paladins, of John Strachey's *Why You Should be a Socialist*, which sold 300,000 copies in 1938. It was also the time when Esmé's grandfather Comrade

Lightfoot, a bright young thing turned Spanish volunteer, knew Palme Dutt, joined the Independent Labour Party and wrote a book of sub-Orwellian reminiscences of his attempt to 'connect', *Tieless in Gaza*. The transition from *flâneur* to potential custodian of the barricades is easily satirised. One remembers Cyril Connolly's lines in *Where Engels Fears to Tread*, a send-up of the career of Brian Howard:

> M is for Marx
> and Movement of Masses
> and Massing of Arses
> and Clashing of Classes.

('It was new. It was vigorous. It was chic!') But in the 1930s it was possible to believe that the Left possessed a constituency of readers and that there was some sort of symbiotic relationship between the two. The interest aroused by a pamphlet such as Nancy Cunard's *Writers Take Sides on Spain* (six lone voices stood out for Franco) could never be repeated now, and in fact was not in 1982, when somebody produced a similar collection of opinion on the Falklands war. It is also possible to believe that this accumulation of opinion, nurtured by Priestley's broadcasts – considered dangerously subversive at the time – and the availability of cheap polemical literature went towards assisting the Attlee election victory of 1945.

So what happened? Why has our own age not produced an Orwell, a Walter Greenwood, a Spender even or a Patrick Hamilton? (*Hangover Square*, published in 1941, is only an averagely good saloon-bar novel but it contains an interesting analysis of the psychology of Fascism.) The explanation lies not in the fact that we inhabit a less political age. Given the radical agenda of the last ten years, given the Falkland Islands, Ulster, the Bomb, mass unemployment, *glasnost*, could any age be more political than our own? It does not even lie in the organised Left's breathtaking loss of nerve. Rather, it lies in the fact that writers have lost the ability to describe and define the society of which they are a part.

Always in the English novel, the traditional English novel with its keen eye for social gradation and its trick of 'placing' its characters, writers achieved their odd, luxuriant plausibility by appearing to understand how society worked, by anatomising the various forces and interests by which its characters were directed. The great writers of the Victorian age could do this. Read a novel like *Vanity Fair* and ask yourself why it tells you so much about the society in which it is set. The answer lies not merely in its patient inventory of detail and artefact – and Thackeray is about the only English novelist from whom you could learn how to order a suit of clothes or discount a bill – but in its ability to link individual lives with the great historical processes. In many ways Thackeray's novel is the refraction of an entire society responding to Waterloo, at once a macrocosm and a microcosm. Occasionally this becomes explicit, notably in the roll-call of historical cause-and-effect at the end of Volume One when Napoleon lands in France, all Europe is ablaze, the funds fall and '. . . poor John Sedley was ruined'. You find a similar perspective in Trollope, a novelist of whom Hawthorne said that he conveyed an impression of a world 'hewn out of the earth and put under a glass case with all its inhabitants going about their business'. At heart, this is nothing more than an analysis of power, a profound sense of *who is in control*. The world which Trollope creates in the Palliser sequence of novels is a complex and mysterious one, but its authenticity lies in the fact that it is explicable. It is run in a formal, political way by Plantagenet Palliser and the Duke of St Bungay, it is owned by the Duke of Omnium and a few snickering cronies, its spiritual well-being is in the hands of Archdeacon Grantley and Bishop Proudie, and that is about all there is to it. It is a coherent world, one might add, in that it is demonstrably not inviolate. Trollope's later work is full of attacks on delinquent foreign adventurers with the potential to disturb this equilibrium. Ferdinand Lopez in *The Prime Minister* with his cargoes of more or less imaginary guano, and Melmotte the gargantuan swindler of *The Way We Live Now*, possibly Trollope's most obvious 'state of the nation' novel, are a looming threat, and though they are beaten off there is a sense that they have weakened and contaminated much of what is left behind.

The Way We Live Now is a convincing analysis of mid-Victorian society, in which a foreign merchant with apparently boundless reserves arrives in London and begins to interfere in its economic and political life. It convinces because, without obvious effort, Trollope manages to draw the contending sections of Victorian society into Melmotte's ineluctable orbit; the speculators who need his commercial backing; the politicians who assist his route into parliament, the hard-up aristocrats who are forced to kow-tow. Finally, when Melmotte presides over a vast dinner held at his house in honour of the Emperor of China, a dinner which coincides with the advent of his downfall, there is a sense that the whole of society has convened to watch his demise and shelter from the fall-out. Yet Trollope's analytical skills were not always displayed on so wide a canvas. Always, he is able to dissect the gradations of the community he chose to write about. There is a telling example of this in a scene from *Barchester Towers*, when old Miss Thorne of Ullathorne hosts her annual *fête champêtre*. The fête is incidental to the plot – its only function is to provide a venue for the usual juxtaposition of Eleanor Bold and her aspirant lovers – but it is strange how the arrangements exercise Trollope's mind to the extent that he devotes a couple of pages to them and constantly looks backward during the ensuing chapter and a half. Initially the arrangements appear to be straightforward: 'The order of the day was to be as follows. The quality, as the upper classes are designated by the lower with so much true discrimination, were to eat a breakfast and the non-quality were to eat a dinner'. To this end two marquees are erected to accommodate these banquets: one for the quality on the garden side of a deep ha-ha, another for the non-quality on the paddock side. However, Trollope then explains that no one who has not had a hand in the preparation of such an affair could understand the difficulties which Miss Thorne encounters in the project.

In the first place there was a dreadful line to be drawn. Who were to dispose themselves within the ha-ha, and who without? To this the unthinking will give an off-hand answer, as they will to every ponderous question. Oh, the bishop and suchlike within the ha-ha and Farmer Greenacre and suchlike without. True, my unthinking friend, but who shall define these such-likes? It is in such definitions that the whole difficulty of society consists. To seat the bishop in an armchair on the lawn and place Farmer Greenacre at the end of a long table in the paddock is easy enough, but where will you put Mrs Lookaloft, whose husband, though a tenant on the estate, hunts in a red coat, whose daughters go to a fashionable seminary in Barchester, who calls her farm house Rose-bank, and who has a pianoforte in her drawing-room? The Misses Lookaloft, as they call themselves, won't sit contented among the bumpkins. Mrs Lookaloft won't squeeze her fine clothes on a bench and talk familiarly about cream and ducklings to good Mrs Greenacre. And yet Mrs Lookaloft is not fit companion and never has been the associate of the Thornes and the Grantleys. And if Mrs Lookaloft be admitted within the sanctum of fashionable life, if she be allowed with her three daughters to leap the ha-ha, why not the wives and daughters of other families also? Mrs Greenacre is at present well contented with the paddock, but she might cease to be if she saw Mrs Lookaloft on the lawn. And thus Miss Thorne had a hard time of it.

This is a relatively subtle analysis of mid-Victorian class distinctions and the antagonisms inherent within them (Mrs Lookaloft does make it on to the lawn and, yes, Mrs Greenacre is mightily affronted). These days, of course, such a grading of place and position would be impossible to accomplish.

How do you 'place' a computer programmer from a four-bedroomed house in Basildon whose father was a bank clerk, or an options trader on £40,000 a year who hails from the backstreets of Rotherhithe? It takes an old civilisation to set a novelist in motion, Henry James once remarked. Alternatively, we inhabit a fragmented, rapidly-changing social climate, a society whose controlling forces are so remote, impersonal and powerful, that it defies analysis. After all, if I stop to consider in whose hands lies ultimate power over me, I am not sure that I can supply the answer. Mrs Thatcher or a man at a desk in America? I live in England, a country administered by the British government, but there are American servicemen in the airforce base down the road. Economically, I am a single unit at the end of a chain of banks, building societies and insurance companies, which are themselves only a part of a global money market.

But in some ways the gap between art and society, between books and life, is more fundamental than this. The 'two cultures' debate, which so animated the critics of twenty or thirty years ago, was comparatively belated, for it ignored the fact that science and the novel parted company nearly a century ago. We live at a time of continuing, astounding scientific discovery, but is there a novelist now writing who can adequately explain the scientific basis of the modern world? Of course not. This is not to assert that the writers of the Victorian age were in some way scientific polymaths – it is significant that Dickens can introduce you to a revolutionary inventor like Doyce in *Little Dorrit* without even troubling to tell you what his invention does – but reading the novels of a century ago, the early Wells and to a certain extent Gissing, you are conscious of writers operating in the vanguard of scientific thought. It is not going too far to say that *Born in Exile*, perhaps Gissing's best book, is nothing less than a debate about the nature of existence. Against the background of Lyell's geological discoveries, its hero falls in love with a friend's pious sister and, as a means of assisting his chances, tries to pass himself off as a trainee clergyman. Eventually he is unmasked as the author of a storming article in a rationalist journal. The denouement with the thoughtful Sidwell is at the same time an emotional crisis and a dramatisation of the crisis between spiritual faith and Huxleyite rationalism.

This is a crude summary of Gissing's novel, but it is enough to show a novelist taking on an entire canvas, dramatising an issue — 'the' issue to many of his readers — without reducing his characters to the level of emotional ciphers. It is not that Gissing is more skilled — in many ways he is a novelist whose fingers are all thumbs — or that he reaches a greater level of engagement with his characters or possesses some magic key to the complexities of human motivation; it is simply that he works within narrower limits. In one way the Gissings and the Wellses understood things because there was so little to understand.

The failure of British writers to cope with their own vast, chaotic canvas looms up from any of those books which still wear their 'awareness' like a regimental tie, those novels in which the most important character lies inert in a silo somewhere in Cambridgeshire and the cast sits around having contrived discussions about the nature of patriarchy. A good representative of this genre might be Margaret Drabble's last novel *The Radiant Way*, commended by Lady Antonia Fraser as an example of political intent in writing (one might also mention *The Middle Ground*, which appeared, serendipitously enough, at about the time the Labour Party started to fragment). *The Radiant Way*, discussed in greater detail in Chapter III, fails on a number of counts. It fails because its author is operating at the fag-end of an elderly tradition and chooses not to see that you *cannot* write like that any more, that any attempt at the panorama effect is bound to fetch up as a queerly narrow perspective. It is also irrelevant in point of style: in other words it is the usual drawing-room chatter, artificial and remote.

At the same time the urge to produce the novel of social comment, the 'condition of England' type book, dies hard. It would be wrong to make too many claims for David Lodge's fiction – Lodge is a parodist who always writes with one eye on the spectacle of himself writing – but no discussion of the novel as social document could fail to ignore *Nice Work*, published in 1988 and a departure for a writer who has spent most of his time outlining the gymnastics of minor academics. Here, according to the blurbwriter, Lodge 'takes as model the condition-of-England novel of the 19th century and causes that neglected prototype to dance to a startlingly modern and infectiously entertaining tune'. It is an ambitious aim, signalled to the reader by epigraphs from Victorian industrial novels, quotations from Dickens, Disraeli and Mrs Gaskell, and, as one might expect from a novelist of Lodge's sensibility and preoccupations, the novel is at much a skit on Victorian social realism as something existing in its own right: a tongue-in-cheek mimicry of Dickensian convention which is strikingly apparent at the end where a *deus ex machina* arrives to offer jobs and futures, and one of the characters unexpectedly inherits £160,000. But the central oppositions, between Vic Wilcox, the managing director of a Midlands engineering firm, and Robyn Penrose, a youngish lecturer in English literature, between industry and academe, are made painstakingly clear, the ironies of their juxtaposition – each is supposed to 'shadow' the other as part of a public relations exercise – dutifully worked out. Penrose, for instance, an expert in 19th-century industrial fiction, reveals that her experience of 'business' is rather less than nothing: in other words her knowledge of the activity which created her own area of study is non-existent. Similarly her leftist views on disarmament are punctured by the relevation that Wilcox's firm, and the workforce it sustains, would cease to exist without defence contracts.

Just as transparent is Lodge's authorial role: that of a self-conscious social registrar. Set in the early part of 1986, full of scrupulously observed detail, *Nice Work* aims for deliberate authenticity. An early description of Vic waking up and prowling around the silent family home gives Lodge the opportunity to bring in contemporary newspaper headlines, followed by an inventory of the house and its contents, even down to Vic 'levering his feet into a pair of highly-polished black calf Oxfords'. This specificity persists as the reader follows him on his early-morning drive to work through the industrial conurbation (scene-setting details from earlier commentators like Carlyle) and continues at work where the dialogue is carefully contrived to bring in references to topical events and personalities ('Look at Sam Fox.' 'Who's he?' 'She. Samantha Fox. *You know.*') Leaving Wilcox at the office of J. Pringle & Sons, Lodge then turns his attention to Robyn Penrose going through a similar matutinal preparation, sketching in biographical details, dress, even turning a knowing academic eye on her philosophy – most of Robyn's life revolves around modern critical theory – of 'semiotic materialism'. It is all neatly done, worked out with Lodge's usual grip of irony and comedy, and sustains a customarily high level of technical accomplishment.

Subsequently Vic and Robyn carry out their shadowing process, provide each other with several eye-openers about their respective jobs and even go to bed together during the course of a business trip to Frankfurt. But none of this adroitly plotted action, the wayside hilarity – there is a marvellous scene in which Robyn explains the metaphor and metonymy of a cigarette packet to her bemused interlocutor – disguises the fact that these oppositions are unusually facile. Such is the gap between Vic and Robyn, between running a factory and 'semiotic materialism', that Lodge can only dramatise it by means of rigid stylisation, as in a scene where Robyn tries to explain her notion of the death instinct in Freud:

> 'Essentially it's the idea that unconsciously we all long for death, for non-being, because being is so painful.'
> 'I often feel like that at five o'clock in the morning,' said Wilcox. 'But I snap out of it when I get up.'

This is amusing, in a gut-level, one-liner way, and it is an effective put-down of academically cloaked statements of the obvious, but it is caricature. In the same way Vic, Robyn and the other characters are not so much attempts at real people as suits of clothes – painstakingly described suits of clothes – which act as repositories for conflicting sets of attitudes. All Lodge manages to demonstrate in this factitious culture clash is a compartmentalisation of modern life whose pockets are impossible to infiltrate. Every so often in *Nice Work* a character pops up with a specific, revelatory function, for instance, Basil, Robyn's merchant banker brother (in fact one could use Penrose-type jargon and say that Basil is a metonym for the City of London), but the only impression conveyed to the reader is that of homework well done. In contrast to, say, Trollope who can supply you with precise data of the details of Melmotte's fall, Lodge is no wiser a huckster in the financial marketplace than any other layman. If anything, *Nice Work* demonstrates the futility of thinking that you can satisfactorily represent in fiction the complexities of life in modern Britain. Not, of course, that this was the author's sole intention: in its analysis of the way in which the rigid principle of Robyn's work and the loose practice of her life fail to match up, the novel is quite as much an attack on the limiting effects of theory. Then again, this spilling over of private academic skirmishes into the wider battleground of fiction is typical of society's failure to provide a centre in which the 'realist' novel of social and political commitment can usefully exist.

III

Some Contemporary Novelists

Kingsley Amis, Margaret Drabble, Ian McEwan,
A. S. Byatt, John Fowles and others

Oh dear, I do have this awful leaning towards the conventional novel.

Margaret Drabble
(quoted in Robert Firchow, *The Writers' Place*)

The English social realist tradition cannot contain the realities of my lifetime, horrors which one might have called surreal if they had not actually happened.

Eva Figes

Among the eighty or so novelists, editors and critics who contributed to *The New Review* symposium, there was only a single major dissenting voice. Malcolm Bradbury's remarks are couched in characteristically apocalyptic tones ('This symposium deals with a topic on which I have such passionate feelings that a brief statement of them will hardly do, but let me try') but they are worth quoting as the enunciation of a view of fiction that gained increasing ground, largely due to the efforts of the indefatigable Professor Bradbury, during the ensuing decade. 'The past ten years have been a striking and outstanding season in the writing of the English novel,' Bradbury wrote, 'and over this period its character, commitment and potential have changed enormously. However, few people seem to know this or take any great interest in it and in critical and commercial forums the novel has been seriously undersold.'

Bradbury was writing ten years ago, of course, but his broad view of the development of the British novel has not altered in any major essential since that time. In fact, a trawl through the critical pieces assembled in *No, Not Bloomsbury* (1987) reveals that his commitment to this upbeat view of British fiction is as impassioned as ever. Bradbury is possibly the most widely read critic in England at the moment, and while you may occasionally deplore his role as a sort of protean *éminence grise* of the novel – reviewer, creator, televisual pundit, Booker judge – what he says is rarely without interest. The Bradbury thesis goes something like this. Briefly, the English novel is surrounded by a depressing and outdated folklore, which assumes a climacteric of around 1940 when Joyce and Woolf were dead and a significant age, a 'high season' in the evolution of British fiction, had come to an end. They were followed, however, by a reaction against experiment, a reversion to provincialism and Little England-ism, an 'I like it here' philosophy (the title of an early novel by Kingsley Amis) which suggested that Woolf, James, Joyce and co. should never have existed. This was a popular view, abetted by journalists, and making much use of convenient tags like 'Angry Young Men' and 'The Movement', and it involved the capture of a great many novelists, writing in a variety of styles, and their imprisonment in a cage marked 'social realism'. Yet by the 1960s a fracture in this easy categorisation was obviously apparent. Many of the best writers who had been brought together beneath this banner – Angus Wilson, Storey, Murdoch, Burgess – had made it clear that their intentions were much more eclectic and wide-ranging (social realism was boring as hell by now). Simultaneously, there had come into being a period of remarkable vigour and innovation from younger talents, 'writers who have, many of them, felt at least the effect of the radiations from Paris and Johns Hopkins or wherever, who have questioned the text they create, who have acknowledged that realism is at least a limited or partial aesthetic; and though such credentials are not automatic guarantees of distinction they have vastly transformed the mood of the novel'.

Did they? Have they? Did anybody notice? I don't think that this summary is misrepresenting Professor Bradbury's views: most of it is assembled in his own words. It is not, perhaps, undervaluing the merit of this thesis to say that it is an attack on easy categorisation that ends up by making its own categorisations. Obviously the social realist taxonomy of the 1950s was absurd (it meant making Iris Murdoch an honorary angry young man), and Bradbury is right to point out the idiosyncrasy of an Angus Wilson or a David Storey. Moving on into the 1980s there are any number of writers who have acknowledged that realism is at least 'a limited or partial modern aesthetic' – Rushdie, Mo, Carey, Martin Amis – though there is the drawback that most of them write from a peculiarly unEnglish perspective. Where Bradbury runs into trouble is with his 'vigour and innovation from younger talents'. Christine Brooke-Rose, Alan Burns and Nicholas Mosley are, it is fair to say, more or less unreadable and more or less unread. To claim that Margaret Drabble and Ian McEwan, two more in the Bradbury list, 'felt at least the radiations from Paris and Johns Hopkins' is to assume a degree of writerly awareness that probably doesn't exist. Unfortunately – inevitably, one is tempted to say – it is of course the *reader*'s fault. 'There is a scene of much aesthetic curiosity and energy,' Bradbury writes at one stage, 'but very little of this is backed up in the critical forum or in intelligent interest.'

Like many academics who engage in the wider world of people who simply want to read interesting books, Bradbury is probably expecting too much, both from his favourite novelists and his readers. No mythical 'common reader' is going to waste his time on a novel like Nicholas Mosley's *Imago Bird*. Equally, no novelist who aims at a wide public and a sustained level of reader interest is going to care much about the lucubrations of French theorists. One of the failures of academic criticism is that it frequently expects everybody to move in the same direction. Another of its failings, perhaps – at any rate on the strength of Bradbury's recent criticism – is to be seduced by an unreflecting zeal. Reading some of the reprinted reviews in *No, Not Bloomsbury*, it is impossible to see them as much more than superior puffs ('D. M. Thomas's is an unusual order of imagination, rare in Britain, Russianised, dense, an imagination that possesses the powers both of pastiche and genuine innovation' is a fair specimen). Set against this is Bradbury's willingness to engage, to involve himself directly in the processes of contemporary literature. Compared to Professor X who devotes five years of his life at the University of Y to writing *Jane Austen and the Bourgeois Ethic*, to be published by messrs Macmillan at £30 and sniped at by perhaps a dozen of Professor X's colleagues, this is a singular achievement.

The Bradbury theory of the 'vitality' of modern English fiction should be able to withstand some sustained prodding. Here is an examination of five members of the late 1970s pantheon – three younger talents (Drabble, Byatt and McEwan); two 'major figures in any comparative international league' (Amis senior and Fowles) – and their subsequent progress. Professor Bradbury himself has gone from strength to strength in the last ten years. But what about his protégés? How did they get on in the 1980s? How did they shape up?

Kingsley Amis: *More will mean worse*

Conveniently for the critic, there is a circularity about Kingsley Amis's career, a sense that the preoccupations of his early work have moved on to become the themes of his ember days. The unkind might say that the thirty-five-year progression from *Lucky Jim* to *Difficulties With Girls* has been no more than a form of rather inelegant running on the spot. At any rate there are strong connections between the young novelist of 1953 and the populist and controversialist of the 1980s (see the 'Sod the Public' articles in *The Spectator* for a good example of the older Amis in full spate), or perhaps it is just that the attitudes have become hypertrophied. At a remove of three-and-a-half decades it is difficult to appreciate the row which *Lucky Jim* caused on its first publication, how it was denounced by Somerset Maugham as an example of yob culture and inspired in Evelyn Waugh a lasting dislike of an author variously referred to as 'Little Kingsley' or 'The man Ames'. In retrospect the fairly innocuous adventures of a junior lecturer at a ghastly provincial university (probably Leicester) read more as a defence of traditional cultural values than the philistine assault that some contemporary critics supposed them to be.

Lucky Jim's interest is at least as much sociological as literary, whether or not one accepts that no book can have a purely 'literary' interest. Incubated in the period immediately after the Second World War and reflecting many of the tensions of the Attlee administration, it is one of those books which say, in effect, 'life's not like that, it's like this' (the remark is Anthony Powell's) in addition to demonstrating just how dreadful certain people, particularly culturally pretentious people, can be. On one level the novel might be seen as a reasonable enough justification of social intolerance. The man whose view of the past and of its cultural life is entirely bogus, whose contact with other people is an habitual, woolly-minded double-dealing, is easy enough to laugh at; when he controls your destiny, as Professor Welch does Jim Dixon's, then, Amis is suggesting, it is time to take the gloves off. *Lucky Jim*'s status as a piece of socially committed writing is also occasionally overlooked in the exultations over its comic potential. Jim Dixon is not only Welch's cultural enemy ('Aren't you going to stay for the P. Racine Fricker?') but his *political* adversary, as in his stage confrontation with Bertrand, Welch's poseur son. 'If one man's got ten buns and another's got two, and a bun has to be given up by one of them, then surely you take it from the man with ten buns?' This type of statement is characteristic of the novels of the early 1950s: there is a scene very like it in *Hurry on Down* where John Wain's hero Lumley gets expelled from a middle-class party on account of his 'red notions'. At the time Amis was a convinced supporter of the Labour Party, later figuring as the author of a Fabian society pamphlet. Other views, which were to bring him notoriety a decade later, were already fully formed: see for instance the discussion of teacher training policy, a prefiguration of the 'more will mean worse' debate, which occupies pages 169–70 of the Penguin edition.

Amid this concentration on Amis's political position, it is very easy to forget *Lucky Jim*'s many levels as a literary text. Below the surface it is a subtle examination of pretence, the wayside hypocrisies and evasions forced on individuals by any sort of social engagement: Dixon going through contrived, formal conversations with his superiors – parodies of contrived, formal conversations – and hating himself for it. On another level it displays a precise and – dare one say it – 'experimental' ear for dialogue. It is also sharply written ('Fury flared up in his mind like forgotten toast under a grill') and bleakly funny. But even at this early stage in his career Amis betrays an uncertainty over his own position. So eager is he to snipe at pretence that he contrives his own masquerade, his own pretence of ignorance. Take this description of Dixon at a university gathering.

He'd read somewhere, or been told, that somebody like Aristotle or I. A. Richards had said that the sight of beauty makes us want to move towards it. Aristotle or I. A. Richards had been wrong about that, hadn't he?

This is plain disingenuous. It is Amis feigning incomprehension, selling himself short intellectually. If the narrator knows enough to throw around names like Aristotle or I. A. Richards, then he knows who actually produced the quotation. And already there are the Little Englander touches, the ritual rubbishing of anything foreign, of modern art, of anything resembling intellectual debate. While much of this is an honest reaction to a great deal of 1950s *New Statesman* trendiness, in which the superiority of the French in any area of life from cuisine to philosophy was an article of faith, it is the bogus insularity of a man who ought to know better and knows he ought to know better.

Much of Amis's progress through the 1960s can be seen to reflect this deep uneasiness over attitude and outlook. Simon Raven wrote an interesting essay in *The Spectator*, marking the publication of *I Like it Here*, Amis's third novel, examining what he called 'The Amis figure', the man at the centre of any Amis novel. It was a poor book, he deposed, because of its author's uncertainty. Having got the Amis figure – ambitious and upwardly mobile – to a position of comparative power and prosperity, he simply did not know what to do with him. The contents of the essay collection *What Became of Jane Austen?* (1971), much of it autobiographical, mirror this indecision. There are the splendid Amis fulminations over cant, the demolition of a great deal of 1960s sophistry, the honest statement of his altered political views ('Why Lucky Jim Turned Right') and a lot of what looks like, well, fake populism.

The older Amis has continued to have his successes, notably with *Stanley and the Women* (1984) and *The Old Devils*, which won the Booker Prize in 1986, although some critics alleged that this was merely a reward for past services rendered. His latest book, *Difficulties With Girls* (1988), with its reintroduction of characters from *Take a Girl Like You*, a novel from the early 1960s, provides a neat perspective for comparisons of Amis past and present. *Difficulties with Girls* finds Patrick and Jenny Standish (née Bunn) lodged uneasily in the midst of the swinging sixties. Though Amis provides his usual sharp dissection of a marriage – Patrick womanising, Jenny trying to conceive – it takes little analysis to establish that this is not so much a book about people, or even a book about changing social mores, but an exercise in punditry. Taking place against the backdrop of the Jenkins homosexuality law reforms and featuring a character named Tim whose 'difficulties' are ascribed by a crank psychologist to latent inversion, it is a fine old display of saloon bar philosophising, taking in nearly all women, most men, homosexuals, modern poetry and its practitioners, educational methods, drugs and any form of behaviour that might remotely be labelled as 'permissive'.

Style might just allow a novel to bear such a weight of implied social judgement. Here is a sample of the late Amis style:

> She considered that as regards what you were born with she had a better deal than most, but she had been behind the door when they were doling out the knack of getting on with the booze. Those who could go through life half-cut were just not aware of how lucky they were.

Cliché, of course, exists on several levels. Used in the manner of a J. G. Ballard it can successfully mock an idle thought process: its lazy formulations can parody a protagonist's own moral nullity. Used in this way it suggests negligent dictation into a tape-recorder.

Examining the wreckage of a considerable career, you can forgive Amis a great deal. You can forgive the punditry – and even the most progressive educationalist approaches the 'more will mean worse' argument with an uneasy glint of recognition. You can forgive the linguistic caution, which proceeds from a quite reasonable assumption that the ordinary reader doesn't like self-admiring mucking around with language. It is a little less difficult to forgive the persistent, bogus anti-intellectualism. There is an eerie moment in *Difficulties with Girls* when Patrick Standish is 'reminded with some force of the moment in the Powell novels when the narrator chap gets no change whatever out of his uncle on asking him if he has news of a former attachment of his who told fortunes with cards, a Mrs Turdley or some such name'. It is the characteristic Amis note. Amis is an admirer of Anthony Powell's *A Dance to the Music of Time* and knows that the woman is called Mrs Erdleigh. Standish, represented in the book as a clever man – a publisher, no less – would know this too. But it suits Amis's purpose to pretend that anything but a cursory acquaintance with English literature is beyond them both. It is a very English spectacle, this, and typical of Amis: the intellectual posing as a philistine.

Margaret Drabble: *A dying tradition*

Margaret Drabble began her career writing quiet, sharply observed novels of middle-class life, their focus invariably the intelligent, coolly perceptive young woman making her way in the world. To read *Jerusalem the Golden* (1967) twenty years after its first publication is to acknowledge the accuracy of its portrayal of a certain type of sub-bourgeois provincial childhood, and its plot, Clara Maugham's progress from an arid Northern adolescence to a 'real life' in the alluring South, is a fair enough reflection of one small redoubt of 1960s reality: the early generation of upwardly mobile women whose destiny was further education, a career and the single life. Similarly, *The Millstone* (1965), the story of a doctoral student who has an illegitimate child, reflects a number of 1960s 'issues', but without losing its detached, ironical tone (it is interesting to compare it with Andrea Newman's *The Cage*, published in the same year, and note Drabble's infinitely greater sophistication).

Even at this early stage there is a sense in which Drabble knows exactly where she stands, not so much in relation to her subject matter as to the whole debate over the future of the novel. 'I don't want to write an experimental novel to be read by people in fifty years, who will say, ah, yes, she foresaw what was coming,' she remarked in a 1967 radio interview. 'I'm just not interested. I'd rather be at the end of a dying tradition, which I admire, rather than at the beginning of a tradition which I deplore.' Spoken at a time when American university campuses were ringing to talk of 'the death of the novel' and it was a characteristic of experimental writers in interview to growl out their loathing of plot, pace and character, this now strikes an unnecessarily gloomy note. There is a way in which the traditional novel of manners and morals has proved surprisingly resilient: after all, as many critics and writers have discovered to their cost, it is still the type of book most people want to read. Equally typical of the early Drabble is a propensity for the social judgement. Rosamund Stacey in *The Millstone*, so circumspect about Elizabethan sonnet sequences, so mature in so many of her responses, can suddenly define one of her acquaintances as 'in many ways rather a nasty young man, being all that my parents had brought me up to despise and condemn: he was a wealthy, well-descended Tory accountant person, clearly set for a career that would be aided more by personality than ability . . . he had a crudeness of judgement that appealed to me, as it was not ignorant, but merely unimpressed'.

This is all faintly redolent of Beatrice Webb: an attempt at egalitarianism undermined by conscious snootiness and an unconscious assumption that society ought to be meritocratic. Roger's real failing is that his success has very little to do with his ability. The tone is very much *de haut en bas*. It is parlour socialism, if you like, a vague, concerned leftist stance always pulled up short by a sort of gut liberalism. One mark of Drabble's writing, even in the later 'panorama' novels of English society such as *The Ice Age* (1977), *The Middle Ground* (1980) and *The Radiant Way* (1987), is that it is rarely *consciously* unfair to anybody – except occasionally to wealthy, well-descended Tory accountant persons.

It ought to be possible to write an amusing parody of the type of novel which sets out deliberately to sum up a decade, which brings a group of people together at some artificial climacteric and attempts to trace the pattern of their connection. Let us say that it is the closing minutes of 1989 in the Hampstead home of Ariadne and Hugo Parmenter, and that a tribe of their acquaintances has arrived to swell the celebration:

> Establishment, bohemian: in the last half-hour of 1989 several of Ariadne and Hugo Parmenter's guests ventured to descry the outlines of what, for them, had been a fractured, miasmic decade: some attempted to speculate for the next. The house was full of pundits, from impresario Simon Tattler and ecologist Mary Greenbank to Eurobond salesman Gavin, alarmed about Japanese depredations into the gilts market, from satellite television boss Hugo Parmenter to microbiologist Ian Stoddart, across whose consciousness the spectre of listeriosis was already casting a wide, frightening shadow: from experimental psychologist Bertrand Eady (who had heard rumours of the effect of inflation on the management of pension funds) to Alison Lovejoy, worried about the security of her own position as lecturer in needlework at a liberal arts college . . .

Then, of course, the scene needs to change. A shift in perspective. A twist in the thread. Ariadne, of course, will have a sister two hundred miles away in some stage Northern town, where, of course, a somewhat humbler but equally resonant celebration is taking place. Thus:

> A quarter of a mile down the road, bonhomie was also in evidence at the home of Harold Grimethorpe, that thin, much disliked, grandfatherly owner of Hinge and Bracket, newly elected governor of a government-sponsored technology college, who believed that the rebirth of manufacturing industries, a promise so long unfulfilled by an ambitious and centralising government, was at last in sight . . .

And so on. And so on. As a matter of fact *The Radiant Way*, consciously set out as a dramatisation of English society at the end of the 1970s, parodies itself. It begins with a New Year's Eve party at the Harley Street home of Liz and Charles Headleand, portentously advertised ('A significant night, at least in journalistic terms, and there would be journalists here this evening, no doubt comparing their own analyses of bygone seventies . . .'), it assembles a varied, heterogeneous cast and then:

> Conventional, unconventional: in the last half-hour of 1979 several of Liz and Charles Headleand's guests attempted to formulate what, for them, had seemed to be the convention of an eclectic, fragmented, purposeless decade; some attempted to prophesy for the next. The house was full of trend-spotters, from gossip columnist Ivan Warner and irritable feminist Kate Armstrong to Treasury advisor Philip, worried about pension projections in an increasingly elderly society: from information vendor Charles Headleand to epidemiologist Ted Stennett, across whose horizon the science fiction disease of AIDS was already casting a faint red ominous glow . . .

Already we have a narrative choked by detail, by the self-conscious accumulation of fact. Then, of course, the scene needs to change. A shift in perspective, a twist in the thread. Liz, of course, has a sister two hundred miles away in the 'figurative' location of Northam, where, of course, somewhat humbler but equally resonant ceremonies are taking place:

> Half a mill up the hill, spirits were also high in the home of Eddie Duckworth, that plump, much-loved, avuncular manager of Pitts and Harley, newly elected President of the Chamber of Commerce, who had faith that at last a government had been elected that would put a stop to inflation . . .

You see the trick? By amassing various different, involved perspectives Drabble is trying to manufacture an overview of the state of England in the dying moments of 1979. But there is a point at which plausible recreation ceases to be plausible recreation and becomes dramatised sociology. Take this description of the guests breezily discussing:

> The approaching steel strike, the brave new era of threatened privatisation, the abuse of North Sea oil resources, the situation of Afghanistan, the Annan report, the prospects of a fourth television channel . . . the disarray of the Labour Party, the deplorable vogue for Buck's Fizz as a party drink . . .

This is simply an inventory. Tom Robinson is singing 'The winter of '79'; the women are wearing Laura Ashley dresses, but that is about as far as it goes. One could contrive a similar accumulation of scene and opinion by bringing together a month's front pages of *The Times*. Moreover, it is difficult not to feel that the cool, laconic Drabble style has disappeared somewhere in the hunt for the grand, panoramic vista.

> Most of them will go: the communal celebration draws them, they need to reinforce their own expectations by observing those of others, by observing who is in, who is out, who is up, who is down. They need one another.

That is almost pleonasm, a characteristic Drabble trick of refining an original thought in such a mild or negligible way that the reader scarcely notices. You could edit out a third of the first one hundred pages of *The Radiant Way* and alter nothing. Again, describing attitudes to the coming decade:

> Not all were anxious, apprehensive, ill at ease. Many congratulated themselves on having found a new sense of purpose, a new realism: after years of drifting, of idle ebb and flow, there seemed to be a current. Tentatively,

some dipped their toes to test the water. Others had already leaped boldly in the expectation that others would follow, that it would prove wise to have been seen to take the plunge first.

This is merely the higher cliché. There is a tendency these days to decry Margaret Drabble as an exponent of the 'Hampstead Novel', the keenly observed study of marriage, morals and affluence among young people who are not really worth writing novels about; but this is to miss the point. The failure of *The Radiant Way*, by no means as bad a book as this selective quotation may have represented it to be, is the spectacle of a canvas which circumstance has made it impossible to paint. Whether we like it or not most modern writers have lost the ability to assimilate much modern experience: a loss that these occasional dramatisings of *Whitaker's Almanack* can only intermittently disguise.

Ian McEwan: *Standing up for the sisters*

Ian McEwan's has not been a fecund career. Three slim novels, two wafer-thin collections of short stories, some television dramas, a film screenplay or two: the output of his fifteen years or so as a professional writer would fill a single, decent-sized volume. This is not to say that brevity has somehow harmed McEwan's career: anyone who has had to sift through the prolix, biennial outpourings of a Burgess or a Murdoch will occasionally tire of the fluent, unwearied pen. Short, understated, their material rigidly controlled, McEwan's novels give an impression of fitting perfectly into the shape which their author chose for them. *The Cement Garden* (1978) is little more than a long short story but an extra fifty pages would ruin it. One of McEwan's strengths has always been an ability to convey information about his characters with the minimum effort or verbiage. The sharp, meagre outlines are sufficient: the chasms of absent detail scarcely matter. There is a sense in which the self-absorbed family of *The Cement Garden*, the remote, abstracted couple of *The Comfort of Strangers* (1981) exist as a single point halfway along a high, invisible trajectory. There is more to know, but in some ways the reader knows enough.

Written in the mid-1970s and published in the collections *First Love, Last Rites* and *In Between the Sheets*, McEwan's early fiction exhausted the average critic's stock of superlatives, so much so that there was talk of new directions and devastating debuts – always a fatal omen for a tyro novelist. At the same time, a number of eyebrows were raised at the bleak, relentlessly worked out subject matter. *First Love, Last Rites*, for instance, contains accounts of incest, the abuse and murder of a child, drownings and much wayside oddity, and McEwan's early career was dogged by media reflection of this alleged nastiness (the BBC cancelled a dramatisation of 'Solid Geometry' after discovering that its principal symbol was a pickled human penis). With hindsight it is easy to say – perhaps a shade too easy – that this early work was over-praised, that it appeared at a time when there was a dearth of comparable home-grown talent, that the voice, so frequently lauded for its originality, is actually the standard, dead-pan, self-parodying modernist voice. (Joyce we know and Kafka we read, but Burroughs, who are you?) Similarly, to accuse McEwan of callowness is to ask whether there has ever been a writer in his mid twenties who was *not* callow. But the early McEwan style had an odd, staccato precision:

O'Byrne walked through Soho market to his brother's shop in Brewer Street. A handful of customers leafing through the magazines and Harold watching them through pebble-thick lenses from his raised platform in the corner. Harold was barely five foot and wore built-up shoes. Before becoming his employee O'Byrne used to call him Little Runt. At Harold's elbow a miniature radio rasped details of race meetings for the afternoon. 'So,' said Harold with thin contempt, 'the prodigal brother.'

On the surface this is a style that allows the author little room for manoeuvre, but within a paragraph or two McEwan is dropping in queer, luxuriant images of the dirty book browsers who 'stir like troubled dreamers' and subsequently 'scatter like frightened fowl'. 'Pornography', whose opening sequence this forms, is typical early McEwan, the tale of a duplicitous vendor of pornographic magazines, a sort of emotional Fascist, on whom two women carry out a hideous revenge. There is a gratuitousness about some of the detail (an old man coughs, 'folding the tissue and its ponderous green contents back into his pocket') but the theme is one which characterises McEwan's later novels. Obligingly, McEwan has always made a habit of flagging the way in which his mind was starting to work: he remarks in *The New Review* that 'women writers seem best placed to use the novel seriously to open out relatively unexplored areas of individual and social experience. It is likely that the best fiction over the next ten years will be generated by the women's movement and its peripheries.'

You can argue about the prescience of this – and it would seem likely that the women's movement has not had quite the effect on fiction which many people assumed it would – but what is not in doubt is McEwan's own position. In some ways he is the first male English writer to hook himself on to the feminist lobby, a progress not without its inconsistencies and bruising encounters (McEwan gives an amusing account of the reaction to his attempt to analyse sado-masochism at a feminist conference). *The Cement Garden*, for all that its plot concerns a housebound family of burrowing, self-absorbed children who conceal their mother's corpse, fits this description in that it becomes, without too much prodding, an examination of sexual identity. *The Comfort of Strangers* is an even more deliberate engagement in the sex war and uncannily reminiscent of 'Pornography' in what happens to one of its male characters in the closing chapter. Yet *The*

Comfort of Strangers is not a satisfactory novel. Your first reaction to this account of Colin and Mary ('this was no longer a great passion. Its pleasures were in unhurried friendliness, the familiarity of its rituals and procedures . . .') vacationing in an eerie, deliquescent Venice is to marvel that a man can appear to write about a woman with apparent objectivity, but the sensation is soon replaced by a feeling that what McEwan has gained in outright commitment he has lost in subtlety and textual plausibility. The differences between The Comfort of Strangers and an early story like 'Homemade' are profound, though it should be said that they work both for and against the author. 'Homemade' is a story about incest: the seduction of a ten-year-old girl by her fifteen-year-old brother. It is also an hilarious send-up of male attitudes to sexuality, so effective that disgust at the incident is replaced by laughter at the satire. When, having completed the act, the narrator soliloquises: 'I felt proud, proud to be fucking, even if it were only Connie, my ten-year-old sister, even if it had been a crippled mountain goat I would have been proud to be lying there in that manly position, proud in advance of being able to say "I have fucked", of belonging intimately and irrevocably to that superior half of humanity who had known coitus . . .' the reader knows that he has stumbled upon burlesque. The serious moral point, the point about how men ought to treat women, succeeds by way of its understatement. Contrast this with The Comfort of Strangers and its self-conscious discussions of the nature of patriarchy – though of course it is a great deal 'better written' – and you might begin to wish that the author had not nailed his colours so firmly to the mast.

The Child in Time (1987) is McEwan's most obviously 'political' book: again, anyone who wanted a suggestion of the way in which the author's thoughts were moving in the interim could have consulted the script of The Ploughman's Lunch or the libretto to the oratorio of Or Shall We Die? ('Will there be womanly times, or shall we die?') Set in a drab, authoritarian future – a conscious projection of the straight leftist view of third-term Thatcherism – it has three main components: the attempt of Stephen Lewis, a successful writer of children's books, to find his lost infant daughter and repair the relationship with his estranged wife; his membership of a government commission on childcare; and his dealings with a former government minister, once his publisher, who is regressing to a state of childhood. In a tangle of quotations from 'The Authorised Childcare Handbook' McEwan's intentions are not hard to disinter. Charles, the publisher turned politician, is a peacock parody of the rising Tory MP. ('I have my mandate – a freer City, more weapons, good private schools.') The commission supplies an opportunity to send up the traditionalist point of view in education ('In general the committee was not well disposed towards a phonetic alphabet. Colonel Jack Tackle of the End Domestic Violence Campaign had said that it sounded like a bloody nonsense'). Elsewhere there are reports of 'riots in a northern suburb', of nuclear submarines nosing out into the cold North Sea. There is nothing wrong with this in itself – hats off to McEwan for mixing it with the politicians – but as fiction it doesn't work. The style, in describing the commission's proceedings, is formal and fatigued: the political debate is sheer caricature, and while it may be that McEwan is sending up the more arid aspects of committee land and the low level of national political engagement, this does not make for an alluring prose style.

By contrast, the novel's informal scenes – particularly those describing Stephen's relationship with his wife, his musings over his lost child, his reflections on his own fugitive past – strike a consistently relaxed yet forceful note. Similarly, the portions of the book devoted to Stephen's conversations with Charles's physicist wife offer a sustained meditation on the individual and time. As an examination of the way in which families function, the novel is masterly. As an examination of the way in which people formally react to political contingency it strikes me as fundamentally flawed. Despite its continual felicities of style and observation, *The Child in Time* has still not solved the question of how far 'politics' can go without irritating the reader or undermining the writer's sense of himself.

A. S. Byatt: *Writing for grown-ups*

A. S. Byatt has written four novels in twenty-five years, the gaps between them so expansive that there seems little likelihood of the sequence begun in *The Virgin in the Garden* (1978) being completed much before the end of the century. The sparseness of this output is not so much the result of contending commitments – Byatt has also featured as a university don, the anatomist of Wordsworth, Coleridge and Murdoch, and as a general cultural pundit – but of a meticulous, formal approach to what the novel demands of the writer. It is an intellectual, erudite perspective and its expression in novels such as *The Game* and *Still Life* seldom makes for easy reading.

Something of this precise, painstaking quality, a sense of conspicuous structures sedulously imposed, an unswerving concentration on the life of the mind, can be glimpsed as far back as *Shadow of a Sun* (1964), outwardly another English bourgeois panorama, but, for a first novel, a work of considerable maturity. Common Byatt themes are already predominant: the tensions of family life, the dislocated adolescent (Anna and her 'trouble with school, after which she had left under a cloud'), the clever man, romantically entangled and intellectually ambitious, who ends up just a little way out of his depth. Above all there is Henry Severell, the self-absorbed, intermittently deranged novelist. The 'writer' is a characteristic Byatt figure: Elaine Feinstein noted in a review of the short-story collection *Sugar* (1987) how often the central consciousness of the story was scholarly or passionately preoccupied with literature. There can be an element of self-consciousness in this – early on in *Shadow of a Sun* where Severell's wife turns over the books in the study, 'Bishop Berkeley's *Siris*, Boehme, Coleridge's *Notebooks*', there is a sense only of marker flags obtrusively raised – but the general air of intellectual engagement is never fabricated.

The cool tone. The quiet observation. One has seen so much of this in English women's writing – in English men's writing for that matter. What distinguishes Byatt from the large number of her contemporaries who began their careers in the early 1960s is perception coupled with deliberate unobtrusiveness, a refusal to settle for casual stridency or the grand scene. This is not to say that she resists melodrama – there are several savage climaxes in *Still Life* – but that she has a sense of the emotional limits within which the average person works. Anna, the disaffected *ingénue* of *Shadow of a Sun*, is a good example of this technique. A lesser novelist would have made her more talented, more confused. Byatt lets her remain ordinary and as a result the portrait has a curious kind of conviction. In much the same way the early Byatt had an ability to build up an emotional situation or a relationship by constructing a context of gestures and looks, a range of premonitory hints, which justified the eventual result. When Anna, reeling away from a Cambridge party, bumps into Oliver Canning, a married friend of her father's, and ends up in his bed, there is no sense of chance having played a role, simply an impresssion of unforced continuity.

It is a measure of Byatt's skill that her sense of how people behave to one another can survive the rigour of some of her characters. The cast of *Shadow of a Sun*, as much as their successors in more recent work, seldom take life easily. 'Can't you just *be* in a place, Frederica?' somebody asks one of the sisters in *Still Life*. 'No. I think. I have to *think*,' Frederica replies with unreflective seriousness. It could be an embroidered text hanging above the bedstead of every substantial Byatt creation, a commitment to the elevated point of view that can occasionally become frightening: one remembers Oliver and his homilies against women's magazines. 'One has *never* time to read that kind of stuff ... there is always something one could be reading that would add to one's knowledge, or give one some insight into things.' This is true, of course, but it could be expressed a little less stridently, with a little less self-righteousness. Such statements, though, go a long way towards defining our own and Byatt's view of her characters. A key aspect of the Byatt atmosphere is the enunciation of a social judgement merely as a part of character definition, rather than to promote a wider social objective. There is an odd moment in *Shadow of a Sun* when Oliver, having been introduced to an undergraduate friend of Anne's, remarks: 'For myself, I can't help knowing that there is one clever, innocent, unsophisticated boy from a grammar school who's been deprived of a whole life because your friend had the money, or the schooling and the initial intelligence, to ensure that he could spend his socially obligatory three years doing nothing gracefully in an educational institution.' This encapsulates the argument against an educational system built on privilege, but in stating it Byatt is not asking us to judge a particular educational system, or even Oliver Canning, but simply to be aware of the aspects in Canning's background that would prompt such an opinion. In the context of the social theorising that characterised much fiction of the late 1950s and early 1960s this is relatively unusual.

This type of, perhaps an appropriate word would be *tolerance*, is enough to hint at A. S. Byatt's ancestry. Set mostly in the 1950s, her fiction follows a tradition of post-war English writing that did not, taking its lead from Lawrence and Orwell, break out into social realism but instead looked back to older and less judgemental forebears. Her strongest influence is Forster: in fact, there is a story in *Sugar* titled 'On the Day that E. M. Forster Died' in which the protagonist, herself a writer, reflects that 'he believed in tolerance, in the order of art, in recognising the complicated energies of the world in which art didn't matter'. This is a neat enough synopsis of Byatt's own position, certainly an adequate description of the sensibility at the core of *Still Life* (1985). The second novel in a 'planned series', its events prefigured by *The Virgin in the Garden*, *Still Life* follows a wide floating cast through the mid

1950s, focusing most usefully on the juxtaposition of two sisters, one married to a Northern vicar, the other negotiating the intellectual and physical challenges of Newnham. Searching to describe the novel's overall effect one could say – and these are all Forsterian characteristics – that it locates a certain English mood, that it explores a certain, again very English resignation in the face of adverse circumstance, that it is good on human quiddity, in such a way that a family ceases to be a blur of faces and opinions, and becomes a collection of recognisably distinctive individuals.

One could say also that it is a novel of contrasts and that the main contrast is not simply between child-bearing Stephanie and lickerish, ambitious Frederica, but between the life of action and the life of the mind. The bookishness persists, sometimes enabling Byatt to pull off sumptuous effects although only at the risk of exclusiveness. Describing an hirsute minor character, for instance, she decides that 'it was a beard that Edward Lear would have populated with parasitic life, a plump thrush, a few quails, a tittlemouse'. For anyone who knows their Lear this is a captivating image: for those ignorant of *A Book of Nonsense* it is surely inexplicable. The same saturated intelligence, a cleverness of private codes and shared allusions, emerges in the dialogue, whose sophistication is a little too hard to believe in or to care about. There is a slightly implausible scene in which Stephanie questions her younger sister's resolve to cast a superannuated school uniform, weighed down with a rock, into the river. Frederica replies: 'Steph, did you *want* an electric tea maker? Do you want to rescue these horrible garments, these symbols of pettiness and niggling, for Daniel to give it to some trampess?' This is not so much over-dramatised as sounding like one of Firbank's empassioned dowagers. If *Still Life* has a weakness it is that conversations like this and much of the talk that enlivens the Cambridge charivari has a false brightness, a forced epigrammatic splendour. This is – apparently – a realistic novel and yet someone like limp, donnish Dr Faber with his resolute asceticism, his habit of reeling off

two-hundred-word cultural critiques at the mildest provo-
cation, could not – does not – exist.

This is an over-reaction, born of the fact that there have
been rather too many novels about clever young people at
Cambridge. At least with Byatt there is a sense of genuine
thought, a feeling of intellectual engagement, instead of the
customarily dreary 'stylishness'. Yet by contrast the scenes of
family life, of what might loosely be called 'human activity',
have a humane, quiet and yet zestful quality. Perhaps it is
simply that a description of Stephanie giving birth, or treating
with Daniel's mother and her brother Marcus (another of
Byatt's disaffected adolescents), has more intrinsic interest
than the sported oak talk about 'life' which is so often nothing
more than a sexual prelude, a stylised mating call.

Quietness. Understatement. Yet an ability to deal with the
big, traumatic moments of birth and death. Perhaps in the last
instance *Still Life* is not entirely a 'realistic' novel, for while
it imposes no value judgements it shows a keen interest in
how value judgements are made, mixed with a small degree
of authorial self-consciousness over the difficulties of the
writing process. Much of this debate about 'seeing' is personified in Van Gogh, whose methods of representation form
one of the book's significant mosaics, but it emerges also in
Frederica looking back at 1950s Provence from the Pound-
influenced perspective of the 1970s, in a wayside discussion
of the human response to landscape: 'There are shepherds in
the Andes who have over sixty words for the colour brown
in the wool of sheep. But they are shepherds in the Andes.
Frederica has words for tea party behaviour and shopping
discriminations in North Yorkshire matrons.' This
investigation – and it is nothing less than a debate about
signification – only surfaces intermittently in the forward
march of the text, but the following paragraph, towards the
novel's close, gives some idea of the importance Byatt attaches
to it:

I had the idea, when I began this novel, that it would be a novel of naming and accuracy. I wanted to write a novel as Williams said a poem should be: no ideas but in things. I even thought of trying to write without figures of speech, but had to give up that plan, quite early on.

Still, it was a brave attempt. It is possible to direct a number of criticisms against A. S. Byatt's work. Chief among them is to say, as one can say of Forster, that it is not *muscular* enough, that there is a pallid lack of substance to some of its characters. Another is to lament the narrow perspective. To borrow Faber's complaint about a modish play he is compelled to see: 'There is no sense of large movements of thought or culture – just personal relations and stage lighting. I am afraid it is a very English production.' One could balance this by saying that in the present circumstances 'large movements of thought' are probably impossible to convey in a novel, or that in any case 'personal relations' inevitably reflect cultural progress. Whatever the merits of this debate, the maturity of Byatt's response is never in question. There are, after all, few enough British writers of whom it can be said that they are writing for grown-up people.

John Fowles: *Presenting the past*

In the late 1960s and early 1970s, when the English novel was being damned for its grey parochialism and its indifference to the new winds sweeping across from America and the Continent, John Fowles seemed the answer to a critic's prayer. Not only did his enormous but tightly controlled fiction appear to address the big issues – The Magus, set on a Greek island and providing a witches' brew of Jung, free will and determinism, was heady stuff in 1966; not only did he aspire to technical innovation – *The French Lieutenant's Woman* must be one of the first English novels to incorporate the alternative ending, but he swiftly developed an enormous international reputation. For a time Fowles was a lord of the American campus, as Golding and Tolkien had been before him, selling millions of paperbacks to a generation of US students. The enthusiasm of Berkeley or Yale was duplicated on home territory. At Oxford in the early 1980s no student intellectual's bookcase was complete without its copy of *The Ebony Tower*.

A decade on, Fowles's early novels are very much of their time. Re-read at a distance of a dozen years the revised version of *The Magus* seems tiresomely 'clever', a work of considerable technical pizzazz, flawlessly plotted, but a book in which the author can be seen brooding above his vast, fictional chessboard, reluctant to let a single character out of his sight for an instant. Similarly, *The French Lieutenant's Woman*, which would have taken your breath away twenty years ago, now looks very much like a period piece: even on a first reading one was conscious of the overweening narrative voice. *Daniel Martin*, the sole novel of the 1970s, has not worn well. Set internationally over three decades and in its author's words 'an exploration of what it is to be English', its central character is a successful playwright turned screenwriter trying to come to terms with an uneasy past and its attendant ghosts. All Fowles's skills are on display here: the luxuriant evocations of scene (the rural childhood with which the novel opens, the boating sessions from 1950s Oxford), the examinations of people for whom 'philosophy' provides not a set of remote abstracts but an actual moral paradigm. Did anyone ever write so well, you wonder, about being young and clever and ambitious, or about first love? Something of Fowles's stance comes across in the preliminary punting scene on the river:

The young man would pass, even today; all except his short hair would pass. But even then her full and folksy mid-calf skirt, the puffs in the short sleeves of the blouse are dated; the colours too bravura, too eager to escape the accusation of blue-stocking . . . and faintly irritating, because such a plea is unnecessary. She is, to use a student cliché of the time, very nubile; has both a sexuality and a distinction, a kind of warm elegance and a conscious- ness of it that is almost an indifference . . .

This is minutely evocative, but there is an omniscience about it, a sense that the narrator and his perceptions – Fowles's perceptions – are rather more important than the subject struggling on the pin before him. Jane, whom Daniel is about to seduce prior to marrying her sister, hasn't a chance: unlike the very best characters in fiction, and despite her knowledge of Rabelais ('*Fais ce que voudras*') she has no life of her own. Throughout the narrative Fowles or Daniel – the two voices are purposely inseparable – are continually dropping in to offer advice or retrospective judgement. When Daniel goes to work in the ailing British film industry, 'a better agent might have told him that he was simply being snapped up on the cheap'. His look-backs are invariably couched in the 'Now I see that . . .', 'In retrospect I . . .' tones. The air of contrivance is reinforced by the witty talking heads ('This is getting rather complicated,' says one undergraduate as the bed looms before them. 'Perhaps it's a long overdue simplification,' says the other. Perhaps it isn't) and the sense that truth, emotion or whatever is occasionally being tailored to suit the whorish demands of language. The first time Daniel is unfaithful to his wife it is with a vacant film star. 'He used to tease her a little, innocuously, and she was too dumb to be dry back, but she liked having her pin-up image gently mocked. It gave her the illusion that she could see through it.' This is only marginally superior to – say – Frederic Raphael, a writer for whom any emotion can be offered up as a hostage to the slick formu- lation. In fact, *Daniel Martin*, with its international media background, its Oxbridge preoccupations, its forced dialogue and wayside cleivernesses, is occasionally a shade too sugges- tive of an up-market Raphael.

The comparison is not an idle one. There is something

about John Fowles's fiction that appeals to the adolescent. This appeal has something to do with the plausible explanations of behaviour, a little to do with the philosophy (for the Jung-men among us) and a lot to do with the sex. Fowles's trick, you sometimes think, is to invest adult life with a greater seriousness than it actually possesses. A good example of this is *The Ebony Tower*, full of conversations that seem to reveal everything and in fact reveal nothing very much at all. There is less in it, as Tallulah Bankhead might have said, than meets the eye. *A Maggot*, Fowles's most recent novel, confirms a number of these suspicions. The setting is the 1730s, which with its shades of Jonathan Wild and Hawser Trunnion might be thought dangerous ground for the novelist. Five travellers are journeying on horseback from London to the West Country: a 'Mr Bartholomew', his uncle, a maid and man-servant, and Dick, a deaf-mute who seems to achieve some form of telepathic contact with his master and remains the only member of the party undisguised. The first section closes with the discovery of Dick's body, hanged, at the spot where the party divided. Subsequently the narrative fragments. A little of it is in the third person, rather more in the form of letters from the lawyer Ayscough to his noble patron, the majority cast as dialogues between Ayscough and people who may be able to reveal what happened.

What did happen? Well, even the shrewd old lawyer is unable to work out precisely what went on in that cave, although it appears to have had something to do with pagan rites designed to cure 'Mr Bartholomew' of his impotence. All that can be stated as fact is that the maid Rebecca, formerly a barren prostitute, conceives and undergoes a religious conversion of the most virulently non-conformist kind. Her step-daughter, Fowles reveals, will be Ann Lee, founder of the Shaker sect, whose humanity (rather than religiosity) he admires. This isn't the half of it, of course. Chief among the novel's many themes is the customary reflection on free will. Bartholomew tells Lacy, the actor hired to impersonate his 'uncle': 'We must choose in many small things . . . but yet must at the end, in great matters, obey.' You are also presented with a modern sensibility's conception of the 18th century: artificial and deliberately so. The contemporary speech is ingeniously done, but in a way that draws attention to its own facility, while the narrative tone becomes mildly officious when describing childbirth statistics or the chemical constituents of Rebecca's make-up. Perhaps the most skilful touches appear in the interrogations, where small facts, let slip unwittingly, illumine wide areas of 18th-century experience: Puddicombe the West Country landlord assuring Ayscough 'I am no fanatick or meeting man'; Lacy describing his career on the boards; the curate bemoaning the lack of intelligent company. But despite the large topics it touches on, *A Maggot* suffers from a lack of narrative purpose. Fundamentally, it tells you more about the 20th-century's reaction to the 18th century than about the 18th century itself. Like the articulate sophisticates who populate Fowles's earlier fiction, it is a recreated past that has no life of its own.

Voices in an Empty Room: *The experimental novel in the 1980s*

Question and answer sessions at meetings of the Oxford University Literary Society in the early 1980s followed an invariable pattern. The celebrity speaker – Margaret Drabble, A. N. Wilson, Lord David Cecil – would retire gracefully from lectern to chair; an audience of fifty or so undergraduates would stir uneasily in their seats; and a polite young woman enquire whether anybody wanted to say anything. Whereupon somebody, usually a middle-aged man with a beard, would clamber to his feet and ask: 'Now that B. S. Johnson and Ann Quin are dead and Alan Burns has stopped writing, what do you think is the future of the experimental novel in this country?' The guest would make various self-deprecatory remarks about his or her inability to appreciate experimental fiction – the middle-aged man listening all the while with the consciousness of rectitude – and the proceedings would then be brought hurriedly to a close.

Even then such enquiries seemed quaintly out of date. The great days of English experimental fiction belong to twenty or even twenty-five years ago. It was then that B. S. Johnson was writing *Trawl* and *Christy Malry's Own Double Entry*, when novels were full of scrambled, neo-Joycean syntax, and from across the Atlantic came like-minded 'experiments' such as John Barth's *Lost in the Funhouse*, which contained larky instructions for snipping up and reassembly. But Johnson and Ann Quin died young. Alan Burns simply gave up. The consequent, purposeful critical neglect of their successors was a pity, for what Johnson – the only major talent – and his attendant zealots were trying to do was entirely reasonable. If you were to ask the average 'experimental novelist' to state his or her aims and intentions, they would probably come out something like this: The average novel, with its certainties and neat formulations, its plots and narrative line, implies a cohesion that isn't actually in the world. It finds order and certainty at the expense of what is so. But all significations are arbitrary, all patterns imposed. And, naturally, conventional ways of writing fiction only magnify the difficulties of conveying truth via the medium of words. For a start fiction cannot be 'true' because it tells stories. All the novelist can do is to attempt to scythe through the carapace of an essentially misleading language to disinter true meaning.

This is a fair enough ambition, even if many of its propositions might be regarded as axiomatic; exposing uncertainties in the writing process which will always remain insoluble. It is still sufficient to motivate a small band of English novelists such as Gabriel Josipovici, Sue Roe and Nicki Jackowska. In addition, there are other, better known writers, for instance Eva Figes and, more recently, Maggie Gee, who started their careers in the experimental corner and subsequently moved out into the mainstream. Abetted by sympathetic publishers

– John Calder and the Harvester Press – the experimental tradition has been kept alive, albeit precariously.

The drawbacks of the experimental novel will be readily apparent to anyone who has ever tried to read one. Students of the homegrown avant garde will recognise all the customary textual signals in Jackowska's *The Islanders* (1987), scenes from the life of a 1950s adolescent who escapes from her sequestered upbringing but is enmeshed forever in the sinewy ties of family. There are the usual considered, elliptical sentences and the usual complete lack of context. Where is the island? Who else lives on it? When does the ferry arrive? These are the sort of questions the average novel reader would want to ask Ms Jackowska and the average novel reader would be right to ask them. This absence of detail is an enduring fault of experimental writing, quite as much as the overblown similes (a Sunday 'like a bale of cloth spread out and shimmering as though patched with gold thread') and the dismal sense of nothing ever happening. But at least Ms Jackowska doesn't go in for the disembodied talking heads, another favourite resort of the avant garde, in particular Gabriel Josipovici:

> What we should do is invent a game.
> What sort of game?
> I don't know. There must be lots of games.
> We've played all the games.
> That's what I mean. We need to invent a new one . . .

You can make what you like of this, the opening lines of a short story called 'Children's games' – my own guess is that it is a metaphor for the fiction-writing process – but the fact remains that no ordinary reader will ever be bothered to make the effort.

Many of the concerns of the contemporary avant-garde are dramatised in Sue Roe's *Estella: Her Expectations* (1982). In some ways this is less a novel than a theoretical tract – significantly, since its appearance the author has confined herself to heavyweight criticism – characters from Dickens's

novel set down in a penumbral feminist environment, in-
exactly defined although the setting appears to be French.
Estella is a dreamy adolescent, Miss Havisham an ageing
dancer. Pip makes a brief appearance as one of Miss Havisham's pupils. The novel's faults are those of every experimental work since Joyce. It is solipsistic and static up until the
final page. The 'highly original' style promised by the blurb
means a lot of sentences without verbs and, when describing Estella's sexual enlightenment, a sort of desperate
breathlessness. The book could perhaps be described as a
reverie in which Estella imagines herself in various female
roles: a French *maman*, a gypsy's doxy, a writer. These are her
'expectations'. Elsewhere, *Estella* emits all the characteristic
warning noises of the experimental text. There is the spirited
tampering with someone else's original. There is the reader's
continual inability to distinguish between dream and reality.
Above all there is an opacity about the proceedings that is
quite deliberate. The confusion inflicted on the reader's mind
is an obvious part of the novel's intent, which is to provide a
debate about the difficulty of conveying actuality through
language. Estella tells Miss Havisham: 'Writing's impossible.
You can only tell stories, that's the problem, if you want
anyone to read it. I wouldn't be able to keep the story moving.
I'd want to write a still life.' This is an effective statement of
the ancient dilemma of the avant garde novelist. Yet even if
you dispense with plot, which Sue Roe does, gleefully, there
remains the difficulty of getting 'between writing and what
you're writing'.

This is true enough, as far as it goes – although you might
want to suggest that language, with all its built-in deficiencies,
is all we have. You might also want to suggest that Ms
Roe's solution, using the techniques of painting to allow a
description of 'the real world of light and fashion, the surfaces
of art', means little more than a greater recourse to metaphor.
Estella's sexual initiation at the hands of someone called
Jonathan is 'a slither, a slice, of the stark, fine light, the fine
lines and breaths of this night, to keep forever on a page'

which is a memorable sentence, but elsewhere a lot of the densely figurative language seems rather slipshod.

There are a number of responses to a book like *Estella: Her Expectations*. One is to point out that formal experiment and reader interest are not necessarily mutually exclusive categories: look at Ballard or, in the pre-war days, the techniques of the early Anthony Powell novels. Another is to say that overdoses of critical theory inevitably vitiate the art of the most gifted writer. Oddly enough, Ms Roe is capable of startling, if more conventional, perception, as in her description of a pub bar-propper who 'when he moved made a tangible absence behind him'. Despite its achievements in a much maligned genre, *Estella* only illustrates the dismal fate of experimental writers in a hostile literary environment: novelists with ambitious aims and tiny readerships, whose books are reviewed as curiosities and sell abominably.

IV

The Literary Establishment and the Middlebrow Conspiracy

We attach much abstract dignity to the Novel, these days, but we do little for those in the practical business of creating novels – provide nothing like an aesthetically vigorous environment or a serious critical measure . . . Seriousness arises as a cultural compact, and the commitment to value must be shared with and by those who sell or discuss, read or criticise.

Malcolm Bradbury

The chief function of the book reviewer is to rebuke the impudence of publishers in laying so much trash before a weary public.

Evelyn Waugh

Though it is sometimes possible to believe that the great monsters of modern literature are entirely self-supporting, no novel exists in a vacuum. Even a Mills & Boon novelette, taped to the back of a soap packet, requires a context in which to function, a sense that there are other soap packets harbouring other Mills & Boon novelettes and that some sort of scale of values exists by which to differentiate, classify and influence: obviously there is a relationship between what gets written about books and what gets written in them. Similarly, though critics have always ventilated the idea of cultural compacts, if not always in such modish phraseology, the context is essentially that of consumer satisfaction. In general books exist to make their authors and publishers money, and to give pleasure to the reader. Consequently, to talk of encouraging 'an aesthetically vigorous environment' and 'a serious critical measure' is to posit a situation which in the context of popular journalism and medium-level cultural debate – the sort of debate which the average fiction reader pays attention to – can never exist. It would be too much, for instance, to expect *The Independent* to devote its entire weekend book section to a radical interpretation of the Victorian novel or a symposium on critical theory, however much 'literature' or some of its guardians might be served by such selectivity. By the same measure it is unrealistic to expect a person who reviews books for a Sunday newspaper or a weekly magazine to apply cogently thought-out critical standards. If the reviewer shows a willingness to discuss books seriously and a liveliness of response, then the review-reader might feel that he is doing his job a good deal better than some of his colleagues.

Any enquiry into the existence of a literary establishment, the standards by which it operates and the efficiency with which it functions, is hampered by the obvious lack of a broadly-based cultural forum in this country. A great many people have an interest in the future of fiction, from Professor X who researches into the *nouveau roman* at the University of Y, to the *Observer*'s weekly fiction reviewer and on to the bookshop browser who buys three hardback novels a year, but cultural fragmentation has meant that there exists no platform on which the three of them can meet without some form of compromise or dilution of standards. Professor X may occasionally review for the *Observer* but he will not do so in the tones he habitually uses to dissect Robbe-Grillet. A fair number of fiction reviewers know something about the *nouveau roman* but this rarely means that the doors of the *Critical Quarterly* or some other academic journal are suddenly open to their work. This situation – academics trying to write down to their audiences, journeyman reviewers trying to write up – often leads to bizarre juxtapositions. It is quite usual to find parallel columns of the *Sunday Times* proclaiming that novel A is 'a witty, reflexive text' and novel B 'a pleasant, relaxing read'.

This is an exaggeration, born of occasional academic cravings for a wider audience and frequent journalistic desires to rise above the Grub Street motley. But it demonstrates some of the difficulties inherent in defining a 'literary establishment' and its usefulness. Another difficulty is that of comparison, a consequence of the eagerness of most writers to dish the dirt on the prevailing literary ethos under which they laboured. In retrospect, the 1930s are the decade of Greene, Waugh, Orwell, Huxley and Powell. But at the time there was a profound conviction that genuine critical standards had almost ceased to exist, smothered by an inept and deferential reviewing establishment. Graham Greene paints a dismal picture in his autobiography, *A Sort of Life*:

> The reviewing of novels at the beginning of the 'thirties was at a far lower critical level than it has ever been since. Gerald Gould, a bad poet, and Eric Straus, a bad novelist, divided the Sunday forum between them. One was not elated by their praise nor cast down by their criticism.

It was not simply that the reviewers of the 1930s were facile. They were also more or less corrupt. Orwell, looking back from the vantage point of 1944, summed up:

> The literary pages of several well-known papers were practically owned by a handful of publishers, who had their quislings planted in all the important jobs . . . Even reputable literary papers could not afford to disregard their advertisers altogether. It was quite usual to send a book to a reviewer with some such formulation as 'Review this book if it seems any good. If not send it back. We

don't think it's worth while to print simply damning reviews.'

It should be noted that this is the view of a maverick outsider who had the greatest difficulty in getting his books reviewed at all, let alone favourably, until 1945, but the evidence against the wire-pullers and the backstairs crawlers of the 1930s is conclusive. It would be difficult not to believe that we have in some measure advanced from this cheery venality, although it is still a habit of small publishers to threaten to withdraw advertising unless a particular book is noticed. It would also be difficult to believe that the amount of space devoted to books in newspapers has not radically increased: a consequence of the recent newspaper revolution has been the expansion of book pages, a matter of supplements rather than columns, and a vastly greater coverage of book-trade totem poles such as the Booker and Whitbread prizes. In the 1950s Raymond Mortimer presided over a couple of pages at the *Sunday Times*. His modern-day equivalent, assisted by four full-time staff, has a twelve- or sixteen-page magazine to put to bed each Thursday afternoon.

But the fact that there is more space for book reviews in national magazines, that reviews are appreciably longer and reviewers given greater elbow room, does not automatically guarantee the health of literary criticism. One might as well expect the state of English football to improve simply because a game is televised each Sunday afternoon. The standard of reviewing and the value of more general comment about literature is a consequence solely of the type of people who write about books, the sort of books they are given to write about and the composition of newspaper book pages: in other words the personnel and the attitudes of the literary establishment.

The English literary establishment – I am assuming, you see, that such a thing exists – is notoriously difficult to define. The very amateurism of book reviewing as an activity abets this lack of coherence: after all, anyone can give their opinion of a book and the 'celebrity review' in which (say) an actor reviews a novel by another actor is a feature of popular newspapers. So the literary establishment has innumerable redoubts: the English departments of provincial universities, an Oxbridge common room or two, elegant houses in Campden Hill Square, cramped metropolitan flats harbouring junior playwrights, gloomy bedsitters in Camden Town containing X the aspirant novelist whose 800-page handwritten manuscript *An Ill Wind* has just come back from its seventeenth publisher and who pays the rent by writing reviews for the *London Magazine*. The link between a moonlighting junior lecturer, between Professor Z who occasionally condescends to notice a book that was not written in the 18th century, between Lady Antonia Fraser and X with his suspicion of 'gangs' and 'coteries' which are keeping him out of print, is not perhaps an obvious one, but there is a link. It is an establishment whose members, though they may never meet (and the literary party circuit is largely the preserve of hangers-on) are all vaguely aware of one another's existence, careers and publications. And while much of it consists of publicists and people loosely connected with the arts – the vague-minded woman met at a party who used to work at the BBC – it is personified, it assumes its characteristic focus, in the shape of the book reviewer.

Book reviewers have always had a bad press. 'Kissing the bums of verminous little lions', was Orwell's description of the toadying which necessarily accompanied any attempt to get your books noticed in newspapers fifty years ago. The resentment is a lot older than this. It goes back to the collection of second-rate egotists in *Pendennis*, to the sad, embittered literary wrecks of *New Grub Street*. Orwell's account in *Confessions of a Book Reviewer* of the typical, fraying literary hack of his own day is well known but it is worth quoting at length:

In a cold but stuffy bed-sitting room littered with cigarette ends and half-empty cups of tea, a man in a moth-eaten dressing gown sits at a rickety table, trying to find room for his typewriter among the piles of dirty papers that surround it. He is a man of thirty-five, but looks fifty. He is bald, has varicose veins and wears spectacles, or would wear them if his only pair were not chronically lost. If things are normal with him he will be suffering from malnutrition, but if he has recently had a lucky streak he will be suffering from a hangover. At present it is half-past eleven in the morning, and according to his schedule he should have started work two hours ago; but even if he had made any serious effort to start he would have been frustrated by the almost continuous ringing of the telephone bell, the yell of the baby, the rattle of an electric drill out in the street, and the heavy boots of his creditors clumping up and down the stairs. The most recent interruption was the arrival of the second post, which brought him two circulars and an income tax demand printed in red . . .

Of course this is wildly overdone: the five volumes which the reviewer has been prevented by 'moral paralysis' from reading are *Palestine at the Crossroads*, *Scientific Dairy-Farming*, *A Short History of European Democracy*, *Tribal Customs in Portuguese East Africa*, and a novel, *It's Nicer Lying Down*. Set against it is the fact that not all hacks are so defatigable. Professor Saintsbury, who reviewed for fifty years, recalled that even in his seventies his fingers twitched with anticipation while untying the latest package of books. Yet despite the stage properties of Orwell's skit – the yells of the baby, the thump of the creditors' boots – there is an element of truth in what he says. The contemporary hack, asked to review four novels (a study of divorce in Kensington, a feminist dystopia, a recreation of the life of Nelson and the confessions of a New York drug dealer) in five hundred words might think that it is uncomfortably close to his own reality.

In at least two important respects literary society has changed since the days of Orwell's downtrodden, nerve-racked scribbler and Gordon Comstock anathematising the Cambridge nancy boys, the 'moneyed young beasts' of the fictitious *Primrose Quarterly*. It has even changed since the days of Cyril Connolly's Mr Vampire, literary editor of the *Blue Bugloss*, who stymied the hopes of so many aspirant novelists. For a start – and this is a development of the last twenty years – it is no longer possible to make a living out of book reviewing. In the 1930s when Malcolm Muggeridge retired to Sussex to concentrate on writing novels he found that it was just about possible to survive on the £5 that the *Daily Telegraph* paid him for reviewing the weekly batch of fiction. On the evidence of Jonathan Raban's *For Love and Money*, a collection of literary journalism with an autobiographical tint, you could marginally conduct this subsistence-level existence at the end of the 1960s. You couldn't do it now. *The Independent* pays £80 for a five-hundred-word review; the *Sunday Times* rather more than twice this. A necessarily anonymous 'Literary Review' at the back end of *Private Eye* might fetch £150. But obviously you cannot write for the *Sunday Times* on a weekly basis. Even the most assiduous hack who writes for three or four papers and haunts literary editors' offices like a ghoul (a characteristic sight in a literary editor's office is the youngish, unshaven man looking over the bulging shelves with faint wistfulness) can only bring in £500 a month, and it is more or less impossible to live in London on £6000 a year.

The second important change – it is probably connected to the first – is in the type of people who review books. Orwell's hack was a thirty-five-year-old who did nothing but review. His successors are on the one hand younger and on the other more heterogeneous. Even if they are full-time writers, book reviewing is likely to form only a small part of their overall activities. This is an important factor in answering the question: who reviews books? Professor Z may swoop down like an aged vulture to carry off the new William Golding, novelist A may be brought in to enthuse over the latest masterpiece by his friend B, but in general the leg-work, the appraisal of those countless first novels which 'show promise', the evisceration of those literary biographies which provide a 'compelling portrait' is done by a group of people in their late twenties and early thirties. While broad categorisations are unhelpful it is possible to identify several 'typical' book reviewers:

Reviewer A is male, aged twenty-seven, and lately departed from Cambridge where he spent five years failing to complete a thesis on Ezra Pound. He is currently resident in a single room of the Islington flat of a merchant banker friend. To support himself he is compelled to work three days a week in the publicity department of an accountancy firm where his main occupation is to correct the grammar of men a few years older than him who earn five times as much money. His cultural pantheon includes Eliot, Levi-Strauss, Barthes and Paul de Man. When not reviewing novels for the *Daily X* he is working on a critical study entitled *Harbingers of Modernism*.

Reviewer B is female, aged twenty-eight, and already a veteran of the London literary scene. At twenty-three, after coming down from Oxford where she edited the *Isis* and was a staple of the gossip columns, she wrote a sexy novel which was a mild *succès de scandale* and got her profiled in *Cosmopolitan*. Now married to a barrister, she alternates breathless eulogies of lady novelists with working on her second novel, provisionally titled *A Passionate Disagreement*.

Reviewer C, also female, aged twenty-six and a variant on Reviewer B, is much more of a literary maid of all work. Her father, a well-known impresario, got her her first job on *The Tatler* where she wrote captions for deb party scenes. Within a year or two she graduated to restaurant columns, liberated-young-women pieces for the *Daily Telegraph* and light reviewing for a Sunday newspaper. Her ambition is to interview Erica Jong.

(There is also a fourth type, Reviewer D, the young woman the literary editor met at a party and mistakenly asked to telephone him, but this will do as a selection.) The most obvious feature of these caricatures is their similar social background. But just as striking is their different relationship to the book they are being asked to comment on. Reviewer A, on receiving a novel for review, will fit it into some private literary framework involving both long-term perspective and contemporary comparison. Reviewer B will do this too, but with a narrower focus, principally involving a collection of modern women writers. Reviewer C, it is safe to say, will be rather more interested in whether the author appeared on *Wogan*.

Of course it is not necessary to have a Ph.d. in English literature to write intelligently about fiction. Neither, perhaps, is it a handicap to be middle-class and white: literary society has always been middle-class and white. Nevertheless, there are immediate reasons for the depressed state of English writing which are intimately connected to the literary establishment and the way in which it conducts itself. Ask any reader of modern novels – novel-buyers or library-goers, not critics – what he or she most dislikes about modern novels and the answer is pretty sure to have something to do with them 'all being the same'. This is not so much a complaint about uninspired plotting as an awareness of the *tone* which invests the modern literary novel. Broadly speaking, with the exception of rare categories like the bank clerk who goes home and writes in the evening, novels in this country are still written by literary gents (or gentlewomen) about literary gents and for literary gents. It would be overstating the case to say that literary society – Professor Z, Reviewer A, the hatful of publicists and party-goers – has created, made acceptable and thereby perpetuated a certain type of novel, but it would not be overstatement to say that the typical literary novel has become stylised to a hypertrophied degree, and that this stylisation is broadly countenanced by the people who sift literary novels for public consumption. You know these books. You can get them at the library: books whose titles bear the stamp of the ironic, genteel cliché: *An Unsuitable Attachment, An Intolerable Burden, Incline our Hearts*; books about bourgeois childhoods, divorce in NW3, about women in Conran dresses fretting over adultery, about – God Save Us All – literary London. Their Oxbridge/Hampstead assumptions, their demure ironies and mannered perceptions, their focus on the gyrations of a bunch of emotional poseurs, are to the reader infinitely reassuring (in that everybody likes to be told what they already know) and infinitely useless.

None of this would matter particularly if books were decently and honestly reviewed in this country. Yet with one or two honourable exceptions the English novel is consistently let down by a deferential reviewing establishment with an engrained reluctance to condemn inferior work. Book reviewing – I speak as someone who reviews about fifty books a year – is a racket, a pleasant and sweetly conducted racket, but a racket all the same, in which everybody more or less knows everybody else and gamely conspires in mutual backslapping. It is important to emphasise at this juncture that the literary world is not *obviously* corrupt. Publishers – never reviewers for some reason – very often make solemn pronouncements about the probity of critics. Here, for instance, is Anthony Blond's *The Publishing Game*:

> The reviewing establishment has been criticised as being cliquey, narrow-minded, prejudiced in favour of Oxford or Cambridge and out of touch with popular taste. It may be all those things; it is also fair and totally incorruptible.

To which one may reply that there are implicit and explicit forms of corruption. Obviously, no one is going to telephone a reviewer and offer him money to write favourably about a particular book. Similarly, few literary editors these days send out novels to a reviewer with the instruction 'not to be too hard on poor old X' (though they may make the job easier by sending the book to somebody known to be well-disposed towards X). But sooner or later anyone involved in the world of books will find that he or she operates by way of a subtle network of compromises, a low-level conspiracy that weakens any attempt at objective standards. You are writing a review of a first novel, for instance, to which the only honest reaction is to say that the author ought to have chosen some other career. But then you remember that you are publishing a first novel yourself in six months' time, and nobody wants to be thought . . . ungenerous. Consequently, you produce the usual persiflage about 'promise' and reach exceeding grasp. The author, who is not a fool, will not appreciate this disingenuousness but at least honour is satisfied. Alternatively, a letter arrives from the *Daily X* (a paper into which you have been trying to insinuate yourself for years) asking you to review the twenty-third production of an ailing senior novelist. It is obvious – both to you and the literary editor of the *Daily X* – that the novel is a pot-boiler, but it is also obvious that the writer is a close friend of the literary editor of the *Daily X*. What do you do? You grit your teeth and send a few phrases like 'triumphant achievement' and 'resounding conclusion to a career' hopping around the typewriter.

There is nothing very wicked in all of this, as Cyril Connolly pointed out half a century ago. Such mild hypocrisy is not exclusive to the book world. Frequently it involves only collusion in a moderate form of puffing. Mutual admiration is endemic to the literary scene: one has only to look at the 'Books of the Year' feature in *The Spectator*, where the sight of Peter Levi extolling P. J. Kavanagh is pretty sure to be followed by the spectacle of P. J. Kavanagh extolling Peter Levi. This is harmless enough. A little less harmless is the habitual polite deference that attends novel reviewing. It is quite usual for a reviewer to be asked not to review a particular book if it isn't any good – an especially cogent reason for noticing a book, you might have thought – and with a few exceptions, making some luckless author the victim of your asperity, is not a practice encouraged by the average literary editor. One could go on. It is possible to rehearse an endless catalogue of complaints against certain literary editors and their staff: that they don't notice first novels, paperback originals or books in translation, that they take little trouble to match up book with reviewer (there is simply no point in sending the new Philip Roth to somebody who hasn't read any of the others), that they indulge laziness. Certainly, the charge of laziness invariably sticks. An extract from the blurb of Stephen Spender's *The Temple*, published in the early part of 1988, goes:

> It is transparently autobiographical, about the experiences of a twenty-year-old Oxford poet on vacation in Hamburg, who then travels along the Rhine; and his spontaneous response to the Weimar world of the bronzed young Germans of his own generation – the Children of the Sun – their friendships, parties, sexuality, naturism, especially the cult of the naked body, and all the gauche hedonism that was about to vanish under the Nazis.

Here is Philip Howard writing about Spender's alter ego in *The Times*:

> He responds enthusiastically to the Weimar world of the bronzed young Germans of his own generation – the Children of the Sun – their friendships, parties, sexuality, naturism, especially their cult of the naked body, and all the gauche hedonism that was about to vanish under the Nazis.

The blurb-transcriber and the reviewer are practically inseparable.

Deference. Idleness. Sheer lack of rigour. Spineless, selective reviewing will never prevent good novels being written or read, but it is not conducive to that 'aesthetically vigorous environment' in which fiction flourishes. Naturally, there are points to be made on both sides. Nobody wants reviewing turned into a blood sport as it was when Lockhart's *Quarterly* reviewers established the principle of the slashing notice. Equally, nobody wants the review pages of newspapers and magazines to be full of endless jeremiads – imagine the stulti-fying effects of a dozen columns of pious denunciation, the sort of sniffish carping that *always* reads as if it were written by people wearing horn-rimmed spectacles. But to balance this is the fact that most readers have ceased to be fooled by reflex deference to particular publishing houses and particular writers, no matter what sort of rubbish they might produce. This is especially noticeable when anybody even remotely celebrated produces a book. One of the more absurd sights of the typical books page is the praise nervously lavished on writers of established reputation who – to put it bluntly – are simply churning it out. Bookshop windows are full of books by people who have not had an original idea in years, but one would never imagine this from the reviews. Anyone who thinks that this is an exaggeration should examine the fuss that attended the publication of John Wain's last novel, *Where the Rivers Meet*. It was a bad book, an embarrassingly bad book, in which a dissection of bygone Oxford dissolved into the standard lament for lost time. People from his publishers could be got, at parties, to admit as much. But Wain, you see, is a Grand Old Man of English Letters and so it was decorously reviewed all over the place.

Coteries, deference, false standards are as old as Gissing or Thackeray or Mrs Leavis's attacks on dilettantism in the first issues of *Scrutiny*. But the reader who buys books on the strength of the reviews is likely to feel vaguely swindled, less able to appreciate the really good stuff. If Kingsley Amis is a comic genius and John Wain a Grand Old Man of English Letters, what does that make a *really* good writer, a Martin Amis or a Timothy Mo? The common reader has an idea that there is talent out there. He would quite like to sample it, but the reviewers scarcely notice first novels so he has no means of knowing where it exists, certainly not in the pages of the *Daily* X where the novelist Y is busy hailing the latest masterpiece written by his friend Z. There is no ready solution to this problem. It is all very well to demand a rigorousness, a greater seriousness, an awareness of context and comparative style. The reviewer given a week, say, to review Don Delillo's *Libra* is rather less concerned with whether it is a Great American Novel than with the likelihood of his being able to read it twice and somehow produce eight hundred coherent words in time to meet Thursday's deadline. In any case, in an age of cultural fragmentation, most reviewers are keenly conscious of their own limitations. As John Gross put it in *The Rise and Fall of the Man of Letters*:

> A critic may well protest that his main business is simply to give a reasoned (or unreasoned) account of his feelings about a book in the language of everyday life. He may take a certain pride in being the last amateur in a world of professionals. But all the same, he knows that there are people who know more than he does about things which he is supposed to know about, and if he has any professional pretensions at all, it is hardly a thought calculated to raise his self-esteem.

The reviewer, then, is a non-specialist in an age of specialists. But for some reason calling in the specialist, the 'professional critic' who 'knows about literature' has never provided an effective remedy. At any time in the last twenty years there has been a small band of academics – junior lecturers from York and East Anglia – steadily reviewing in the national press. Leaving aside their occasional consciousness of being a cut above Grub Street – and Grub Street, let it be said, is a cut above Grub Street these days – the sight of academics reviewing modern fiction nearly always presents a depressing spectacle. This is not solely because of the humourlessness

— the reviewer who when confronted with a comic novel calls it 'a text of playful irony' — and the customary neurosis of the specialist performing in front of an audience of non-specialists, but largely due to the anxieties of the critic who realises that reviewing new fiction may force him to drop one set of deeply cherished values in favour of another. This is only to say that whatever theories or views of literature the critic may have knocking around in his head, they are rarely sustainable when set against a contender for this year's Booker Prize. The resultant loss of nerve can be deeply unsettling.

Something of this anxiety is evident in the work of David Lodge, a novelist-academic who has intervened more effectively than most in the wide cultural environment, a man who turns up both in the *Observer* and *Essays in Criticism*. Writing in the preface to the essay collection *Working with Structuralism* (1981) Lodge suggested that a more honest title might have been 'Living with Structuralism'. In that statement the enthusiasm of the critic, who applauded a new expository tool, and the resigned acceptance of the novelist, who realised the implications for his art, were combined. In most of Lodge's literary excursions, notably those collected in *Write On* (1986) there is a fretful battle going on between two types of critic — theorist and enthusiast — with the latter hinting that what the former says is undermining his position. This is an exaggeration, perhaps, but structuralism, the whole of the post-value school of criticism, provided Lodge and his professional colleagues with a set of rigorous analytical techniques, the techniques of sign and structure and system. So what does Lodge have to say within the confines of the middlebrow book review about the writers he really admires? Joyce? 'All human life is there.' Salinger? 'Economy, delicacy, artful mimicry.' In other words, see any critic since Saintsbury. Venture a little further, to the spectacle of Lodge examining his own fiction, and the battle becomes even more obvious. 'In the last instance,' he comments, apropos some deconstructionist nostrum, 'I can't go along with this radical decentring of the literary text. It simply doesn't answer to my experience of writing a novel.' In other words, however brilliant the critic, whatever his ability to dissect a text and dismember the artifice that is fiction, sooner or later a phrase like 'artful mimicry' will be the reader's only honest reaction to the book.

You can sympathise with Lodge the critic and Lodge the enthusiast in their predicament. You can sympathise with the book reviewer whose knowledge of these dogfights in the intellectual empyrean comes only from hearsay. You can sympathise even with the hack given a week to review a potential cornerstone of modern literature. But in this fragmented atmosphere – an atmosphere of young Turks trying not to offend, editors trying to do favours, academics fighting their own interior battles, elderly crowdpleasers fighting for space – the young British novelist is perhaps entitled to feel that most people have lost interest in whatever task he is trying to accomplish.

In any case this failure of the literary-critical establishment adequately to serve its creators is only a symptom of a much wider malaise: the resolute refusal of people in positions of cultural power in this country to take culture seriously. Highbrow-baiting, of course, is a time-honoured national parlour game and it is not at all surprising to find that it is alive and flourishing once more. It is even less surprising to find that the people responsible for its renaissance are journalists. But make a quick survey of the arts pages of the national newspapers and squeezed up against reviews of dull biographies and snobbish *belles lettres* of the *Harpers & Queen* variety, you can be reasonably confident of finding an article maintaining that Proust isn't worth reading or that Salman Rushdie is a fraud.

This type of intellectual deceit, which manifests itself in a truculent incomprehension of anything that might be described as artistically new or different, is a persistent feature of the English literary scene. You could detect it in the pronouncements of the late Miss Marghanita Laski on the contemporary novel, you can detect it in the editorials of the

Literary Review, in the enlightened young people who seek to explain critical theory to the readers of Sunday news-papers. Increasingly it can be descried in the newspaper attacks on 'intellectuals', on querulous writers who decline to support Mrs Thatcher, on pinkish film makers who persist in depicting Britain as an 'authoritarian rat-hole' to use Hanif Kureishi's phrase. On the face of it these assaults on the type of writer who signs an advertisement in the *Guardian* look like a political quarrel, the unconsidered reaction of the Right to woolly-minded liberalism, but the disagreement runs deeper than this. It is a symptom of the much broader dislike of 'cleverness', however displayed or expressed, which has been a feature of English cultural life for decades.

Oh, la fatigue du nord! As an example of the type of mental approach I am trying to define it is worth examining the response to a book like Charles Osborne's *Giving it Away*, which appeared two or three years ago. These memoirs, the apologia of a former director of the Arts Council's literature department, attracted some legitimate criticism in the national press if only because the impression that emerged of their author was desperately unengaging, but it was noticeable that most reviewers reserved their spite for a fairly minor episode in Osborne's career: the amounts of public money lavished on an ambitious but financially unsuccessful literary magazine: *The New Review*. Even today *The New Review* plays a disproportionate role in the middlebrow demonology. What else is there in British cultural life that so infuriates its critics? A modest list would include all literary theory, most of the novels that have the misfortune to be selected for the Booker Prize (how the journalists gnashed their teeth over *The Bone People*!) and anything that might be described in the most remote terms as 'Modernist'; a queer aversion for a movement that is as dead as the Dodo. One grows used to the sort of weary threnody which surfaces from time to time in the pages of the colour supplements. Proust? Unreadable. Joyce? Driven mad by his own vanity. Eliot? Sounded the death knell on English poetry. Neither are the modern masters particularly safe. Kingsley Amis, in the course of a discussion of genre in *What Became of Jane Austen?*, makes a typical comparison:

> Most contemporary novels are like spy novels with no spies or crime novels with no crime, and John D. Macdonald is by any standards a better writer than Saul Bellow, only Macdonald writes thrillers and Bellow is a human heart chap, so guess who wears the top grade laurels?

By *any* standards? Precisely, it's a sentence written simply with the intention to annoy. The flipside of this particular stance – which ultimately leads one to claim that the late Sir John Betjeman was a major poet – scarcely bears contemplating. Assemble in your mind a list of the most memorable novels of the last ten years: *Midnight's Children, The Name of the Rose, Waterland, Life: a User's Manual.* Well, the middlebrows hated them all. Even now the little residue of opprobrium that accumulated around the Booker Prize, slightly diminished by the recent elevation of crowdpleasers like Amis senior and Penelope Lively, has still not entirely diminished. In fact the recent establishment of the *Sunday Express* fiction prize can be seen as a conscious counterweight to much highbrow excess.

There is nothing very new in this peevish belittling of intellect. Always in England if you had the type of brain that was capable of understanding T. S. Eliot's poetry or Kant's logic, you could be sure of finding large numbers of people who would hate you violently for that dexterity. Yet it is important to realise in this grinding quarrel about artistic standards and the trumpeting of spurious talents that the literary journalist, the sort of person who turns white at the mention of French criticism and who thinks that Barbara Pym was the Jane Austen *de nos jours*, has got a point. For one thing it is unquestionably true that in this country the words 'avant-garde' have become synonymous with the worst sorts of silliness associated with artistic excess, and generally the flyblown tribe of 'experimental writers' deserves everything it gets. Though you might question their motives it would be difficult to disagree with certain detractors of *The New Review* who maintained that it was full of feeble poetry and bad fiction which nobody read (though McEwan, Drabble, Shiva Naipaul and Nadine Gordimer appeared there). Certainly there are academics in the reviewing establishment who forget that most books are read merely for enjoyment, and who is there who has not felt slightly sick after reading a *Guardian* arts review?

But to admit that the disillusioned reviewer of Mr Gabriel Josipovici's latest opus has got a point or that a great deal of modern writing is derivative rubbish is to leave a larger question unsettled. After all, it would be fair to say that if Mr Josipovici's readership were assembled in the Albert Hall the ice-cream salesmen would have a pretty thin time of it. More alarming is the sight of critical teeth-gnashing and breast-beating applied to the sort of book people actually read and buy. To say that the latest experimental text from the Harvester Press is more or less unreadable is a statement of fact. To make the same point of, say, *Midnight's Children*, is to call one's own motives as a critic seriously into question.

I dare say that if it were possible to eviscerate the average middlebrow critic the words 'readability', 'plot' and possibly 'tradition' would be found engraved on his or her heart. The depressing thing about most highbrow baiters, the editors who always give preference to some dim biography of a literary hostess over an exotic novel, is the genuine seriousness of their views. It is this conviction, the notion that people like to be 'entertained' (ie amused) and 'but it isn't *funny*' and half-a-dozen other dreary nostrums, that imparts such languor to the lists of books they think are worth reading. Every so often a sort of cry goes up around the byways of Bloomsbury and echoes gently through the columns of the literary journals: it is the cry, a full-throated yet complacent exhalation of the middlebrow journalist who imagines that he has chanced upon the next big thing. A few adjectives such as 'sensitive' and 'delicate' are thrown about and there you are. One sometimes looks at the catalogues offered to the public by publishers each year and thinks: just who are these people trying to fool? In no other branch of public life, perhaps, is it possible for a mediocre talent to go so far simply because of the efforts of a handful of well-meaning nonentities. Occasionally this mass rallying around the flag of modest competence reaches quite exaggerated heights. The admiration lavished on the novels of the late Barbara Pym, for instance, has been entirely out of proportion to their slight but genuine merit. Miss Pym, who died in 1980, was a worthy and, at any rate towards the end of her life, popular exponent of the English spinster novel, a purveyor of sly wit and agreeable malice. Yet A. L. Rowse took it upon himself to extol 'the best novelist of her generation', her books come garlanded with the glowing tributes of Lord David Cecil and A. N. Wilson and the general effect is to make the reader feel mildly unwell. Miss Pym's frail talent is not really up to this anthemic celebration.

Does any of this really matter? The existence of what could be called a middlebrow conspiracy in the arts has a number of implications. It is very easy to talk about abstracts like 'cultural impoverishment' but such an attitude denies breathing space to anything new or artistically different, to anyone who questions the prevailing orthodoxies. More dangerously, it leads to the sight of newspaper editors hot in pursuit of liberal intellectuals and ever ready to gloat at their discomfiture. Quite a number of people emerged with no credit at all from the Salman Rushdie affair, but I doubt if you could find a more disgusting spectacle than the response of Mr Peregrine Worsthorne in the *Sunday Telegraph*:

> Salman Rushdie's apology may well reduce the danger to his life. But it won't remove it, and it is ironic that someone who was only recently inveighing against Mrs Thatcher for having created a police state should now be compelled to rely on that same police state to save

his life. As a result of this experience perhaps he and his friends will come to realise the debt they owe to the practice of phone-tapping, since without that right the security services would never know where to look for would-be assassins.

It is difficult to believe that this was written while a man was going in fear of his life. But it was all of a piece with accounts of 'little Salman, lost in his humourless self-importance as the "great writer"': the fact that a man had been condemned to death was considerably less important than the fact that the establishment had finally got a liberal intellectual within its sights and was avid to let him have it with both barrels.

On a less important level the existence of this type of attitude in Fleet Street and the deeper waters of the literary reviews means that certain types of books tend to get reviewed at the expense of others, those books composed by people who fail to realise that you *cannot* write that type of novel any more, that the complexities of the present age demand a less compliant response than these amiable chronicles of middle-class angst. It is not that the novel currently lacks rigour, or a moral sensibility, or an awareness of the broad themes, or a willingness to mix artistic styles: it is simply that many of the books which do possess these qualities are dismissed by literary pundits as irremediably serious. Until that situation changes you are probably better off reading the latest women's magazine serials – which are usually written with genuine vigour and liveliness – than the current crop of 'literary novels' greeted with such enthusiasm in the pages of the national press.

V

Finding a Voice: Modern American style

Interviewer: Have you found any professional criticism of your work illuminating or helpful? Edmund Wilson, for example?
Waugh: Is he an American?
Interviewer: Yes.
Waugh: I don't think what they have to say is of much interest, do you?

Evelyn Waugh, interview with Julian Jebb,
Paris Review

First, a small diversion. Here are two extracts, each from a novel published within the last ten years: the first written by an Englishman, 'one of the country's leading young novelists'; the second by an American described as 'a novelist of high seriousness and depth'.

There were several other evenings like this. She had not fully predicted the beguiling way in which Barry would admit to being a bit of a poof. It quite turned her on. One night in the disco she found that the hot, bouncy atmosphere of the place failed to match her mood: its smoking; its gyrating; its shouting; its wiggling; its bumping and gesturing. She was surprised at herself. She loved dancing and enjoyed showing off to the fellas. On this occasion, instead, after only a short time on the dance floor, she put her arms round his shoulders and yelled into his ear 'Why not let's go somewhere a bit quieter — you know, back to your place or something?

A. N. Wilson, *The Healing Art*

Trouble was Felisha couldn't stand silence. She needed to be talking or needed Wally talking to her. Riding that perfect body was the only way to shut her up. Then she was as quiet as a church on Monday. Not a peep out of her. No heavy breathing; no sighs or moans or groans. Stillness perfect as that lean-hipped, pillow-bosomed, every-pubic-hair-in-place body like none he'd ever seen before or since. Quickest, stillest bitch he'd laid. Like the whole time I'm fucking her, man, the chick's lying there listening for a phone to ring in Cleveland. You know. A real important call five hundred miles away so she's steady listening, man. Don't intend to miss that call. Quiet like that. I wanted to hurt the bitch sometimes. You know.

John Edgar Wideman, *Reuben*.

Inevitably, it will seem that comparison is ridiculous. Wilson is a white, English, upper middlebrow, versatile performer in a number of literary media. Wideman is black, American and a university professor. Wilson is writing about a girl who works by day in a hairdressing salon attending a disco in Oxford. Wideman is writing about Wally, a basketball scout turned demon avenger of his race, contemplating the body of his girlfriend somewhere in America. But it takes only a cursory examination to reveal that in fact both Wilson and Wideman are trying to bring off the same worryingly difficult trick. In each case the clever, articulate novelist is trying to reproduce the thought processes of a considerably less than clever and articulate character, a reproduction that involves explicit mimicry of contemporary speech. *Mimicry*. Wilson ('it quite turned her on') doesn't habitually write using these lame formulations but he knows his characters might think in them.

Reproducing contemporary speech is the novelist's greatest terror mostly because it can't be done. A faithful reproduction of contemporary speech, printed as spoken, would be ineffably tedious, full of 'ers' and 'ahs' and gormless reiteration. All one can do is aim for a stylised consistency that uses the twists and cadences of everyday speech but doesn't bore the reader and seems authentic in terms of the character and the situation. How do messrs Wilson and Wideman get on? Well, Wilson has an ear for popular cliché ('a bit of a poof', 'turned her on', 'showing off to the fellas'): the 'or something' tacked on at the end is characteristic. But having established the ground-rules, Wilson does nothing with them: no metaphors, nothing resembling an image, and to imagine that popular speech doesn't harbour images is to avoid listening to popular speech. More obviously, it is not one style but two: the mimic style in which the character might be supposed to speak and think, and Wilson's own genteel locution ('she had not fully predicted . . .', 'failed to match her mood . . .') The sole attempt at a flourish, within this sharply defined context, is the smoking, gyrating, shouting sequence which does at least inject a rhythm into what would otherwise be a random assemblage of sentences.

Contrast this with Wideman's loping evocation of the black dude style. At first it seems that *technically* nothing much has changed. There is still the shoulder-shrugging cliché ('shut her up', 'not a peep out of her', 'you know'), the same sexist slang about 'chicks'. But then look what Wideman does with it, stripping away 'thes' and 'thats' to give the sentences tightness and an underlying staccato rhythm, using a few quiet stylistic tricks – the reiteration of 'no's' and 'nots', even bringing in metaphor and simile – 'riding that perfect body', 'as quiet as a church on Monday' – but without losing authenticity. Only a third of the way in does the consistency briefly falter when *ersatz* Wally goes for the 'stillness perfect . . .' comparison that sounds nearer to *echt* John Edgar Wideman. Apart from this minor lapse the excerpt stands as a tight, vigorous piece of prose, composed of contemporary demotic speech and admitting into the text no perceptions which could not reasonably be associated with the narrator. It is authentic (or rather mock-authentic) in a way that Wilson's game pastiche is not.

Later on in the novel Wideman, in the guise of a black girl's lesbian lover, tenders some advice: 'Some Romeo gets your nose open and your legs open. Next thing you know out comes this sweet little cuddly forget-me-not. Then you really got something to keep your mind occupied, twenty-four hours a day, sugar. And where's daddy? Out in the street being lover boy again. You home studying the mailbox. Hope the welfare check come fore the man kick you and baby both out in the street.' *Reuben*, full of these *schlepping* rhythms and dark humour – this, of course, is a book about what it means to be black in a white man's society – goes some way towards solving one of the great conundrums of modern fiction: how to retain the satisfactions of thought and wit and paradox while also dramatising 1980s street language, in other words matching the reader's idea of what the novel ought to be while reflecting the way in which the people out there really speak and act.

Any sort of comparison with America is, invariably, mutually injurious. In the 1970s, while the English novel (with a few exceptions) confined itself to sniffish studies of adultery and coy self-examination, its American cousin flew off out of the window. The fall-out from this dazzling orbit, undertaken by, among others, space captains Pynchon, Barth and Doctorow, continues to descend in the shape of the gallant overplotting, tricksy prose and resolute self-awareness that characterises much modern American writing. At the time this approach was not universally commended. Kingsley Amis supplies a common early 1970s perspective in Firchow's *The Writers' Place*:

> I think that one of the reasons why, according to me, the English novel has got it over the American novel at the moment is because of English snobbery and English conservatism and English class consciousness and all that

kind of thing. Because I think that all this so-called wave of modernism has hit the English novel less hard than any other kind of novel.

Worse luck for the English novel, you might think. But fifteen years ago, as a reaction to work like Pynchon's *Gravity's Rainbow*, this sort of insularity was understandable. There is a sense in which some of the modern American masters have backtracked on their early ambitions, or failed to move on from earlier positions. John Hawkes, for instance, responsible for a much-quoted remark about plot being the enemy of the novel, is on the evidence of a book like *Whistlejacket* virtually accessible these days. Alternatively, Barth's *The Tidewater Tales* seemed a curiously old-fashioned novel in 1988, formless and self-besotted, full of narrative lines that were never taken up and carrying a gigantic sense of its own importance.

In any case the Barth–Pynchon–Doctorow axis is only one aspect of a bewildering variety of modern American approaches. All along the lone, lorn sands of the modern American novel the row-boats of style lie drawn up. There is the black dude style; there is mazy concentration in the North-East; there is tough wisecracking out West; in the big-city lofts there is the amoral, affectless rap of the brat pack. What distinguishes these varied styles is their ability to build on existing resources. Invariably, examining the chunky, under-reviewed American novels that get published in the UK – and there is a whole strain of American writing from Abbey to Hoagland that is merely ignored in England – you find yourself in the presence of writers working within established conventions – the road novel, the novel of the Deep South – and yet producing something that defies obvious classification. To take a luminous example, the heavyweight American political novel, the hollering, God-bless-my-soul-suh epic in which the president claps his hand on the hero's shoulder and the corporation collapses owing to a misunderstanding with Jimmy Hoffa, has occupied a series of American novelists from Upton Sinclair to Marquand. It is a very

American genre this, a category demanding lofty degrees of insider knowledge and conviction, and one which demonstrates the gap between an art form interested in sidelights and half-tones and one capable of confronting what are known as 'major issues' without provoking shrieks of laughter. Only Jeffrey Archer, you feel, could write the homegrown equivalent of a book like John Gregory Dunne's *The Red White and Blue* and the result would be – is – dismal.

The Red White and Blue, a knowing account of a wealthy, influential family caught up in a couple of decades' worth of top-level American history, succeeds by way of its plausibility. It is a gauge of Dunne's achievement that when his protagonist, Jack Broderick, stands for election to a svelte gentleman's club, naming Hoover, Eisenhower and Nixon as his sponsors, the effect is not to inspire eyebrow-raising disbelief but a curious sense of conviction. Throughout the novel – the memoirs of a maverick survivor of the family wreckage – that note predominates: a knowing, streetwise intelligence that can handle the money, power and sex themes without fawning, as if a genius had somehow scripted an episode of *Dynasty*. At its conclusion, when Jack's radical priest brother gets wasted, there is even a presidential intervention:

'I want you to know, John, and I want the American people to know, this administration will not tolerate this kind of mindless violence.'

In the background at the other end of the line, I thought I could hear the whir and click of flash cameras and suddenly I realised that this telephone call was a photo opportunity, and the reason why Dan Corcoran had trotted out his fancy diction. 'That is most reassuring, Mr President.'

'It is a stain on the national escutcheon.'

I saw Fritz roll his eyes.

'It is indeed, sir.'

'Well, then. John, you have my deepest sympathies, and of course Terry's.'

'I can't thank you enough for calling Mr President.'

'You are most welcome, John.' At the other end of the line I could hear the voice of a presidential aide ordering the photographers to leave the Oval Office.

This extract gives you some idea of the several, contending levels on which *The Red White and Blue* exists, and the eclecticism which informs it. Dunne is consciously parodying the style of the publicised presidential intervention – Reagan on the phone to the family of a hostage, Carter smiling his off-centre smile. But both Broderick and the president are gleefully entering into the mockery themselves: they are enjoying the mimicry of gesture which they know the occasion demands, while remaining aware of its inherent worthlessness. So Dunne is parodying two people parodying something which is itself a parody, while still investing the scene with a deliberate air of authenticity. The style is neither realism nor out-and-out satire but something more complex, a subtle skit on reality: a burlesque of twenty years of American history taking in the idiot presidents, Hollywood, Nam, radical politics, gutless hedonism and tinseltown values. It is a send-up which simultaneously sends up its own interior premises, and its effectiveness as a socio-historical register derives from an awareness of the *paraphernalia* of American life. Most novelists avid to record social minutiae would simply tell you that a woman tipped out the contents of her handbag. Dunne will inform you, straight-faced, that it contains two Max Factor lipsticks, a Hershey Bar and a box of See's chocolates with the soft centres pressed in. The bit about the soft centres is characteristic – a dab of superfluous matter that reminds you of the comic specificity of Dickens or Thackeray. The novel succeeds in a number of ways – as a result of its insider awareness of the processes of life and its contemporaneity, but also because of its apparent refusal to take itself seriously. It has all the old charms of plot and pace, incorporates some modernist trickery but without causing the reader to scurry away in bewilderment.

In much the same way the novel of the American South still manages to retain its defiant, ageless quality: like the knife which has had two new blades and three new handles, it seems endlessly capable of renewing itself while remaining exactly the same. Sturdy little bigots stride confidently down the dusty sidewalks, illicit love affairs unfurl behind the closed shutters, communities are rent asunder by random violence, obsession and revenge. On the surface a novel like Pete Dexter's *Paris Trout*, with its racial violence and small-town infidelities, seems no more than a dilution of Faulkner and Styron, but – as with John Gregory Dunne – it is the strength of the narrative voice, in *Paris Trout*'s case approximately five narrative voices, which enables Dexter to survive these obvious comparisons. The novel's central thread is straightforward. Trout, a brooding storekeeper-cum-usurer, shoots a couple of innocent negro women while he is out collecting debts. Subsequently, as a corrupt and negligent judicial process creaks into action, he becomes a single point of light illuminating a web of sneaky evasions and unspoken compromises. A tribe of local bigwigs deplore what Trout has done but can't afford, politically or socially, to let him go to jail.

Again, Dexter achieves his effects by producing third-person reportage which reflects the mental processes of the characters he is tracking around the sprawling heart of the 1950s Georgia dustbowl. In the opening sequence fourteen-year-old Rosie Sayers, soon to be blown away by Trout's shotgun, is confronted by a rabid fox:

> She stopped cold in her tracks, the fox picked up his head. She took a slow step backwards, and he followed her, keeping the same distance. Then he moved again, and seemed to sway. She heard her own breathing as she backed away.
>
> The movement only seemed to draw him, something drew him. 'Please, Mr Fox,' she said, 'don't poison me. I be out of your way, as quick as you seen me, I be gone.'
>
> She knew foxes had turned poisonous from her

brother. Worse than a snake. She stopped again and he stopped with her. Her brother said when the poison fox bit you, you were poison too.

The fox rocked his head and she began to run.

This is skeletal, idiomatic but still fertile ('you were poison too'). A similar approach informs the portrait of Trout, a terrific creation constructed out of tiny fragments of dialogue. 'You sure you want to do this thing boy?' he wonders when Henry Ray signs up for the Chevrolet. 'Onct you make a deal with me I get my money.' Charged with murder he is implacable. 'What they gone do arrest me for collecting legal debts?' These two statements are sufficient: the man is defined. It is an incidental, revelatory technique which reaches its high point in court when Seagrave, Trout's lawyer, stands up to address the jury. First he tries to remember which of the jurors owe him a political favour. Then he glances down at the notepad placed in front of his client. Trout is drawing cartoons of ducks shooting guns at each other. It is a tiny episode but vastly revealing, nudging the reader's shoulder about one aspect of Trout's interior life, conveying the possibility of a judgement, but not, in the last instance, making the reader's decision for him.

English novelists have always been exercised by the problem of idiom: the solutions have been varied. Orwell made the point that Pip in *Great Expectations* speaks conventional upper-class English in spite of being brought up by Joe and Mrs Gargery, two characters with broad Essex accents. Orwell himself invested the lowlifers of *Down and Out in Paris and London* and *A Clergyman's Daughter* with a form of stylised Cockney. With the breakdown of regional accents and a greater homogeneity of phrase and diction the problem of the modern English writer has been made much easier and at the same time much more difficult. Everybody speaks in much the same way but this doesn't solve the problem of reproducing their speech on the printed page, let alone the problem of generating a convincing narrative. In many ways the writer who veers closest to this mimicry of 1980s demotic, or a certain aspect of it, is Martin Amis. *Money* is dominated by a single voice belonging to its narrator, John Self:

> I didn't attempt anything else that day. I drank the drink and ate the grub. I had a shave. I had a hand-job, closely structured round my last night with Selina. Or I tried. I couldn't remember much about it, and then all these guys came walking in on the act ... So me and my sore tooth throbbed our way through a few hours of television – I sat flummoxed and muttering like a super-annuated ghost, all shagged out from its haunting, through sports, soaps, ads, news, the other world.

Amis's use of demotic is wildly idiosyncratic. He creates his own slang conventions ('sock' = 'flat', 'rug' = 'hair' – had *you* ever come across them until you read *Money*?) and then works within them so painstakingly that it convinces. The reader has never met John Self (no great loss, perhaps) or anyone remotely like him, but nobody could doubt that he actually exists. In the same way a number of Dickensian grotesques exist not despite their transparent awfulness and hypertrophy, but because of it. But this cannot disguise the fact that the narrative voice is inconsistent. This is a character-istic of the Amis voice. Take this excerpt from *Success* in which Terry Service, a quasi-yob in the grand Amis tradition, reflects:

> When I said that pathetic thing to Gregory and stumbled down the stairs, whose face burned the hotter with embarrassment and remorse? Mine, mine. Why? I'll tell you why. Because I have no pride, and they merely have no shame.

In the context of the novel this is a stunning moment of self-revelation, but the narrative voice isn't that of Terry

Service, who wouldn't be capable of this type of formulation: it's the voice of Martin Amis. No one, not even the configuration of Dickens and Esther Summerson in *Bleak House*, has ever contrived a solution to the problem of the narrative voice, this glamorous trick of seeming to allow a character to speak for his or her self, of fashioning an *authentic style*. A. N. Wilson's difficulty, as represented in the extract from *A Healing Art*, is that he hasn't the ability to distinguish between contending voices. Amis's 1980s voice is too clever to allow the problem to get in his way. Rather than attempting to solve it – a process in which he possibly isn't interested – he merely uses the discrepancy (between the Amis character and Amis) as another comic vehicle. This is hilariously demonstrated in an episode towards the end of *Money* in which John Self remembers the occasion on which his father put £19,000 on a horse:

> Jack knifed over the whisky bottle, Barry listened to the radio commentary in closing-time light. Sure enough, Bumboy came lolloping out of its stall, each leg going somewhere different, neighing and dumping in its blinkers and Dobbin hat. Eventually flogged into submission by the jockey, Bumboy set off after its vanishing playmates. The horse received the odd joke mention from the commentator until my father smashed the radio, finished the whisky, and suffered a near-fatal nosebleed.
>
> Barry has since acquired a video recording of the race and still gloats over it now. Bumboy not only won, it was more or less the sole survivor. There was one of those churning, drowning pile-ups at the penultimate jump. Bumboy tripped snorting through the chaos – and was clear with one fence to beat. The lone horse pranced flimsily on. It didn't leap that last hedge: it just munched its way through . . .

This is Amis leaving aside any consideration of the narrative voice and going all out for the joke. The reader, by this stage, couldn't care less whether the master of ceremonies is John Self or the author. Amis's novel is a number of things – an examination of an attitude, a gut-wrenching practical joke – but it is also a skit-on-a-skit-on-a-skit, an infinitely layered text, but with a plot, a set of characters and a resolution. For these reasons *Money*, random, eclectic, streetwise, is a key 1980s fiction – one of those novels that help to break through a specific impasse, simply by showing that it exists.

Interlude

An imaginary conversation between Henry James, Anthony Trollope, Ronald Firbank, Kingsley Amis and Professor X of the University of Lyons, author of Radiguet à Robbe-Grillet: l'artifice et l'audace.

JAMES: . . . A perpetual harmony of style, a practised refinement of sensibility: to remove these from the, alas, so rudimentary vehicle of our art would be to withhold from it the felicity of a settled benediction. Yet if I allow myself to address the question of *subject*, I confess that the indecency of the proceedings revolts me. It is as if one were to demand of some poor wanton the secret of her cadaverous charms . . .

TROLLOPE (belligerently): Two young people in love with each other, that's my idea of a story. Two young people out in the hunting field. The girl who marries for money when she should have married for love. The old woman who encouraged it to spite her. And a comic turn with the widowed aunt and her two suitors. That's what made me my money.

FIRBANK: Dear Anthony. So . . . so . . . *bourgeois*.

AMIS: And what's wrong with being bloody bourgeois? Novelists aren't bourgeois *enough*, that's the trouble. I'll tell you a decent plot. A bloke and a girl get married. The girl wants babies. The bloke still wants a bit on the side. The girl spends all her time at home talking to the snooty neighbours. The bloke goes down the pub with a lot of arty-farty poets. Real life. That's the sort of thing the writer ought to write about.

TROLLOPE: Did you ever hunt?

FIRBANK (dreamily): Once . . . after butterflies.

PROFESSOR X: But we should define our terms. 'The writer'. 'Real life'. Are these not in fact dangerously misleading concepts?

AMIS: If you want my opinion, I should say that it was all bloody modernism's fault. Go and ask the ordinary bloke what he wants in a book and he'll tell you: a bloody good story with a plot and some sex and not a lot of nancy boys spouting about art. Isn't that what you'd like?

TROLLOPE: I should like a novel based on sound liberal principles for a change. Something in support of Mr Gladstone's administration. Disraeli has set us all a deplorable example.

FIRBANK (giggles): *I* should like a glass of absinthe.

JAMES: Mr Firbank has the true artist's temperament. He has wholly suborned his personality to the demands of his art. That he has no personality is perhaps a matter of lesser importance.

PROFESSOR X: I must confess that I fail to understand this English preoccupation with 'temperament'. Surely the requirement is to concern ourselves with the text. After all, is it not the text which creates the writer?

AMIS: So who is it puts the bloody words on the paper then?

JAMES: When one thinks of the books through which one has laboured, patiently, sedulously, with a humble sense of what is the critic's duty in such circumstances, only to find that the poor soul has a simply *feminine* conception of literature: a matter of peeping, quivering glimpses into some dimly perceived and nebulous accretion of the elements, then one fears that the descent of pens into hands incapable of grasping them may have had less than satisfactory consequences.

TROLLOPE: Application. That's all you want. A thousand words an hour. Timed by the clock. Breakfast at eight and then start the whole business again.

FIRBANK (simpers): There are the *naughtiest* stories in Maeterlinck. Though they say that he was really a perfect dear.

PROFESSOR X: Not to mention the problem of the erasure. What, after all, is a text except a process of exclusion? It is in silence that we may find significance.

AMIS: You mean what I don't say is more important than what I do? Crikey!

JAMES: Yet one must admit that there are materials which were better unused. An absence of discrimination surely betokens a flagrant disregard of the artistic point of view. Mr Hardy's rustics: they may divert, they may impel us to shed a silent tear, but is not there a *grossness* about their want of elevated feeling?

TROLLOPE: You can't beat a rural wedding to round off the comic sub-plot, that's what I say. The girl gets the man, the gossips get something to talk about and everyone is content.

FIRBANK: *Ugh*!

AMIS (gloomily): Sometimes when I'm bloody bored, which is most of the time, I read some of this new stuff they keep sending me. Blowed if I can make head or tail of it. In my day we knew what we were writing about. Girls, jazz and bugger the Tory government. But that's all changed now. Sometimes I thank God for Mrs Thatcher.

PROFESSOR X (brightly): Once we acknowledge the lie, the inconsistency, we admit the truth. To write that 'the beautiful girl walked into the room' is to beg insoluble questions, to suggest a multitude of definitions. Consider the confusions created by the word 'beauty' in the mind of an English bourgeois . . .

AMIS: And education's at the root of it all. Everything went wrong when they told the thicks about free expression.

TROLLOPE: . . . Followed by a hard day's work at the Post Office and a ride to hounds. Nobody ever wrote anything that he didn't sweat over.

JAMES: To educate? To beckon? To coax? A sacerdotal function is, I confess, not one which I would readily relinquish. But we must be selective. To encumber one's creations with mere *detail* would be to risk an imperfect portrait.

FIRBANK (reminiscently): *I always had one on the frontispiece. Something by Augustus John or Nevinson. Mama rather liked it.*

The voices fade

VI

Outside the Whale

Most of life is so dull that there is nothing to be said about it, and the books and talk that would describe it as interesting are obliged to exaggerate, in the hope of justifying their own existence.

E. M. Forster, *A Passage to India*

How did the Cricks outwit reality? By telling stories.

Graham Swift, *Waterland*

Summaries of the literary situation invariably have a slightly phoney ring to them. No power, Percy Lubbock once reflected, can keep a book steady and motionless before the reader, giving him time to examine its shape or design. If generalising about the specific has its own built-in fraudulence, then generalising about the general is to magnify some painfully obvious hazards. Moreover, there is a way in which what can usefully be said about the position of the novel in English culture has already become a commonplace. We all know that literature counts for far less in a society with a vastly greater number of cultural preoccupations: careful analysis of a bygone age is likely to assure us that it failed to count for very much in the first place. Many critics, tracking the path of the novel from Dickens and George Eliot to Bennett, Galsworthy and Wells and thence to post-war social realism with the moderns thrown in as a sort of unfortunate accident, presuppose a debasement in style, ambition, a sense of what the novel can do. But then debasement is a relative term. It takes no more than a read-through of *Cranford* to reveal that many Victorians thought Dickens vulgar. When Yule, the veteran man of letters in *New Grub Street*, writes a gloomy essay on the corruption by journalism of classic English prose, a yearning for the mellow cadences of Jeremy Taylor is balanced by the thought that for an example of classic English prose corrupted by journalism you need only to turn to *The History of Mr Polly*. To suggest that Wells's influence is corrosive is to ignore the self-renewing nature of language.

And notions of debasement and decline mean very little to the 'common reader', the person who accounts for the majority of library borrowings and bookshop purchases, and has only a hazy conception of what may be critically fashionable. Classics aside, most people read books with very little sense of chronology. To say that the novel has 'declined' is of only passing interest to the casually selective fiction reader whose concept of literature is a mosaic composed of various random shards. Then there is the drawback that popular taste, the books which people *prefer* to borrow and buy, lags twenty or even thirty years behind the fashionable taste and may never catch up. Reading the unpublished and unpublishable manuscripts sent to literary agents – a job which most critics undertake at some point in their careers – can be a salutary eye-opener. The books which the great reading public wants to write and see written are invariably dense, rambling family sagas and adventure epics: the models are not Amis and Drabble but Cronin and Delderfield. What the cultural theorist knows as 'taste' will always be fragmented in any advanced society: applied to a category as all-embracing and variously appealing as the novel, this can make a nonsense of the idea of dominant strains or interior compartments. The highbrow, who looks down his nose at the books reviewed in Sunday newspapers and reads Umberto Eco in the original, is one aspect of this divide. At the other end there are plenty of people who take Jack Higgins seriously and only a cultural snob would mock them. Within this wide arena of different readers responding to different books, the problems of the 'literary novel' can seem to be of very minor importance.

Too minor, perhaps. No doubt, as a Marxist critic would say, culture is 'ordinary'. There are consolations in populism and it is very easy to sneer at a solemn review of a 'serious novel' in the knowledge that it may only sell a thousand copies. But then, in the age of the satellite dish, the VCR and insular leisure, it might be argued that an enduring popular culture, in the conventional sense of the term, has almost ceased to exist. Marshall McLuhan, one might feel, was not a wholly accurate prophet, and the medium has not become the message in quite the way that he envisaged, but a great deal of what passes for culture these days is instantaneous to the point of non-existence. The serious novel may have its own problems in assimilating the chaos around it, but as the pace of the mass culture increases it is one of the few sober indices that we have available.

Inevitably this line of argument can look like special pleading. Justifying the novel's existence is one of the more pointless critical preoccupations. People, one can safely assume, will always read fiction, even if that fiction – judged by one set of critical standards – is not particularly good. From this perspective public obituaries of the novel can seem dangerously removed from reality; doubts about the factors affecting its production and reception equally misleading. A pot-boiler by an elderly crowdpleaser will always be politely reviewed; a great deal of youthful talent will always be ignored; 'reviewer' is all too frequently synonymous with 'backscratcher'; Grub Street, however well-swept the cobbles, will always be Grub Street. There is also the increasing pressure on an art form forced to compete in a marketplace of contending public attractions and demands for editorial space: paradoxically the hype and the outrageous puff and the celebrity interview (Mortimer on Kingsley Amis, James on Barnes) do at least ensure that fiction gets noticed among a riot of more casual diversions. But the pressures imposed on criticism by this battle for breathing-space are enormous, so much so that book reviewing can often degenerate into a process of picking winners, seeing significance in items of limited value, overpraising out of a desire not to seem negative. The appearance of a writer of obvious but not remarkable talent, an Anita Brookner or a William Boyd, is likely to place the average reviewer under considerable strain, the suspicion that *Hôtel du Lac* is simply a superior English spinster novel, that *A Good Man in Africa* is simply Amis-and-water, balanced by an acknowledgement of genuine merit. In these circumstances it is difficult to avoid making extravagant claims for a novelist which hindsight will probably not support, and the literary scene of any decade will always be littered with the bones of great white hopes of the novel who were unable to sustain critical expectations.

The point could be made of the 1970s. Amid this critical confusion, amid the uncertainties of an art form all too prone to revealing its own vulnerability, it is hard not to feel that we have improved on the situation outlined in *Fiction and the Fiction Industry*. The 'Americanisation' of the English publishing scene, seen as an inevitable progression a decade and a half ago, has been broadly resisted in everything except ownership. The literary prize syndrome, for all its faults and its fêting of senior writers for past rather than present achievements, has seen a number of complex but rewarding novels gain an exposure that might otherwise have been denied them. Television channels retain their book slots. Watching a novelist on *Wogan* may inspire only contempt for the unthinking punditry and the facile self-congratulation of the proceedings, but it is a triumph – a *survival* – of a sort.

At the same time, to dwell on the deficiencies of the literary scene is to ignore the existence of a new strain of English writing whose effects have been profoundly felt, and resented, over the last ten years. The names are familiar: Martin Amis, Graham Swift, Timothy Mo, Peter Ackroyd, James Kelman. It is not that there is any overriding connection between them – and to talk of 'new strains', as people did of the Movement or the Angries, is nearly always to tumble into the trap of bogus categorisation – but that they are unlike the traditional hierarchies that preceded them. The difference between, say, *Money* and *The Radiant Way* is enormous, although both writers are trying to perform what is essentially the same trick. Similarly, James Kelman has the same working-class roots and preoccupations as a Sillitoe or a Chaplin: it is only the perspective and the form that have altered. If anything unites these novels, if there is any single factor that establishes a link between Martin Amis and Kelman for instance, it is an eclecticism, a defiance of categories and a willingness to use whatever writerly styles and techniques may be necessary to achieve the overall effect. Trying to 'place' a novel like *Money* is more or less impossible. Part of it might be described as 'realistic'. A lot more is surrealist burlesque. Any lurking conviction in the reader's mind that this is a plausible recapitulation of plausible circumstance is quickly replaced by an acknowledgement that the writer is interfering: significantly Amis himself appears in the text chatting to his hero, John Self, about the processes of fiction. In much the same way Kelman's *A Disaffection*, a week in the life of an embittered Glasgow schoolteacher, is a scrupulous accumulation of fact and detail, but the technique is stream-of-consciousness, with odd, mad interludes where reality and fantasy are inextricably combined.

To locate a new eclecticism in English writing is not, perhaps, to suggest a sea change, and it is not even to say that it is a prerogative of new, younger writers. Novelists as various as J. G. Ballard and Angela Carter have always pursued this approach with varying degrees of success. Even in older writers of established preoccupations there is often an intermittent realisation that, in describing new and unfamiliar circumstances, the old forms will not do. David Storey's *Present Times*, for instance, a novel about a middle-aged man's attempt to come to terms with changing social mores, is notable for its willingness to burlesque as a means of getting over the inherent absurdity of what it is trying to describe. Listening to the protagonists' daughters mouthing their radical clichés, or the speeches made at a parent–teachers' meeting held at a school of progressive educational views, you are conscious that not only would no one ever speak in this way, but that Storey is aware of this discrepancy. Only *haute* stylisation can get across his notion of prevailing cant. This was not a technique that characterised novels like *Savile* or *This Sporting Life*. *Present Times* is a 'realistic' novel which uses non-realistic methods to achieve its effects. On a much more deliberate level this conflation of styles, objectives and intent is evident in a book like Julian Barnes's *Flaubert's Parrot* – both a novel and a piece of literary criticism – or Ackroyd's *Hawksmoor*, which is both historical recreation and, in its varying plinths of engagement, a parody of a parody of a parody.

Searching for an adjective to describe these types of novel one emerges, inevitably, with the word 'fabular'. *Money* might be described as a moral fable of the late 20th-century Anglo-American landscape, the type of book in which the author tells a number of small lies in order to emphasise a large truth. A feature of much 1980s writing, particularly the Commonwealth strain exemplified by Salman Rushdie and Peter Carey, is this obsession with telling stories, indulging in any sort of fabrication or artifice if it can be seen to assist the forward motion of the text. Herbert Badgery, the 139-year-old hero of Carey's *Illywhacker*, will feed you his opinions on truth and lies, reality and subterfuge, at the drop of a hat. After all, 'it was no trouble to lie'. No. This sort of revelation, that sort of symbolic game being given away, is quite deliberate – a hint to the reader, requiring only his own decoding, a warning about the likelihood of artifice and dissimulation. Forewarned, forearmed, we stride on into the text.

One should not make any radical claims for Carey. The open-armed acceptance of artifice is a central force at work in the modern novel. More advanced forms of critical theory demand that each book exist as its own meta-text, endlessly commenting on its own preoccupations and resolves, turning in on itself to demonstrate symbols and inconsistencies. From the reader's point of view this is a mixed blessing. The intermittent feeling that one has broken in on the author's private codes, risen to a higher level of interpretation, perhaps, than the creator anticipated, can be stimulating. At the same time one can pine for the sense that the author, like you, is waiting breathlessly to see what will happen to his characters: an older but slightly less dishonest form of artifice. One can forgive the author as puppet master. It is a little less easy to forgive a puppet master who, masochistically, wants you to see the strings.

Australian fiction was always a likely candidate for this approach – a consequence less of modishness than historical circumstance. Carey has drawn attention to a comment by Mark Twain on the confusing and downright implausible nature of much Australian history: presumably this can be taken as a defence of his own method, which is to write equally fanciful fiction. You can't, after all, truthfully explain the inexplicable. The connection is made explicit in *Illywhacker*, itself Australian slang for 'confidence man' and a role Badgery gaily entertains from the moment in 1919 when his Morris Farman lands at Balliary East and introduces him to the entrancing Phoebe McGrath. A brief married idyll ends after her elopement with Horace, the travelling poet, whereupon the novel fast-forwards to 1931 when Badgery, seven years on the road with his precocious offspring, encounters Leah Goldstein, a dancer of obstinate virtue attempting to support her maimed husband. As Badgery and Goldstein Theatricals they traverse the 1930s 'like flies on the face of a great painting', to use Carey's memorable phrase, until Leah returns to her husband and Herbert ends up serving a ten-year stretch in Rankin Down gaol . . .

This is only a restrained summary of the first section of a vast, diffuse plot full of luminous characters and incident, but already something of Carey's intention becomes apparent. Subsequently, throughout the progress of 'Snake Boy Badgery', his role in the Great Victoria Mouse Plague and the establishment in Sydney of the world's greatest pet emporium, it is possible to detect unflinching ulterior motive. 'Illywhacker' is Carey's metaphor for fiction, 'a trickster, a ripperty man, a conman': underlying the novel is a debate about truth and fiction. Badgery contends that lies enliven. 'You call it a lie. I call it a gift.' Throughout *Illywhacker* a ragbag of unfocussed events is given connection and design by symbolic coat-pegs negligently distributed through the text: the snake, for instance, which makes a pivotal appearance early on. Badgery, determined to impress Phoebe, tells her that it's a pet, a deceit from which much ensues. The result is a comic novel and something more: confronting the reader on one hand with a sensation of stories falling off trees on either side of the path, each demanding investigation and comment, on the other a sneaky manipulative continuity, a panoramic awareness of past and future contingency. But, significantly, *Illywhacker* works on several levels. There are the consistent pleasures of Carey's prose style – an old man's skin hanging from his arm 'like a roast chicken wing', an umbrella attack on Badgery's aeroplane which does no more damage than 'a knife in water' – but there is also the sense that this interweaving of form and content is being used to illuminate a whole country. Watching Badgery's dealings with his canny, self-assured countrymen, noting his complaint that 'the country is full of bloody salesmen', one can also speculate that 'Illywhacker' is a metaphor for the Australian past.

If *Illywhacker* demonstrated some of the rewards implicit in this type of writing – the sturdy prolixity, the mundane grandeur – *Oscar and Lucinda* drew attention to some of the risks. The tale of an odd, Victorian cleric with a passion for gambling who travels to Australia, falls in love with an heiress and enters into a crackpot scheme to ferry a glass church off into the outback, provides a similar mass of themes and symbols of which glass and gambling are only the two most prominent. Again, there is the fabular touch, a sense that each episode exists as a square in a quilt of reinvented history – the early scenes, in which Carey reconstructs the childhood of the son of a Victorian naturalist-cum-religious extremist, are a reworking of Gosse's *Father and Son* – the continual focus on objects. A kitchen stool, hair, glass, the Christmas pudding which Oscar's father casts into the fire. Each of these properties leads cunningly back into the narrative. It is an oddly *filmic* technique, like the fight in the Western saloon that begins with shots of objects being flung through the swing doors, or the avant-garde love scene that starts with a slow pan across the bedroom ceiling.

Returning to Australia, however, to depict Lucinda's early life in the dustbowl of New South Wales, the story turns oddly static. Unusually for a discursive, 200,000-word novel this is not the fault of the plot, which saunters carefully along contrasting Oscar's shabby life at Oriel with Lucinda's purchase and edgy superintendance of the glass factory. Rather, it is a question of focus, a suspicion that *Oscar and Lucinda* has more perspectives than it can reasonably be expected to sustain. At the same time Carey's theory of characterisation, which succeeded in the elaborate, luminous grotesques of *Illywhacker*, here seems mildly suspect. Oscar, with his nervy piety and his unerring knack of backing the favourite, Lucinda with her queer resolution and her own gambling addiction, Mr Ferris the bizarre clerk turned expedition leader: they are engagingly strange, but stage strange. Their quiddities, on which the book's impetus depends, are cosmetic. You cannot imagine having a conversation with Oscar as you could with Swann or Pierre Bezukhov: you would only stand and stare. That wondrous sense of inner fires, steeply banked, which you get with the very best faked existences is absent. By the time the reader reaches the novel's climax and the glass church floats down the Bellinger river, there is a feeling that Oscar, Lucinda and their attendants have been left some way behind.

The writing, of course, is flawless: exact but without lingering over its own facility. 'Death came at him like a ghost in a dream,' Carey writes of Oscar's youthful forebodings, 'one minute cold and wet like his father's oilskin, so he shrank from it and cried out in his sleep, pushing the tight-banded flannel sheet into the pit of his stomach, and then sometimes it was warm and soft and wore the unfocussed smile of his mother.' But wayside brilliance can only take the reader so far. Does *Oscar and Lucinda* work as an historical epic? No, because it lacks any substantive context, any idea of what is going on elsewhere. Does it work as a fable? Not quite, because there is a randomness and an obliquity about the proceedings, a hint of excess detail that is merely excess detail. Fables might create their own context, work by their own set of rules, but the process demands a devious exactitude from the author. It is the principle that separates *The Lord of the Rings* from C. S. Lewis or Stephen Donaldson or any other fantasist that you care to name. There is a sense in which *Oscar and Lucinda* is a great, flimsy edifice, radiant with light but structurally dodgy and pervious to cracks – rather like Lucinda's glass church. And that, of course, ends up at the bottom of the Bellinger river.

Not all Australian fabulists are as successful as Carey. It is possible to mess this up, as a novel like Rodney Hall's *Kisses of the Enemy*, an overblown portrait of an Australian dystopia, amply demonstrates. In a limited way the fabular strain has its outposts, its borderland sentinels in exclusively English writing: in lapel-grabbing moral fables, books in which, set against the chaotic backdrop of the late 20th century, or its parodic extension, people get told *how to behave*. *Success*, an early Martin Amis novel, in which two fairly unlikeable men, one the other's foster brother, undergo a pitiless role reversal to the point where the second even nails down the first's job, is a scrupulous catalogue of moral evasions and deceits. *Dead Babies*, Amis's second, scarily mature, work, is more deliberate even than this. Monitoring the progress of a clutch of youthful hedonists through a wrecked weekend, it is an explicit condemnation of the 1960s liberal ethic, the sophistries of free love and 'liberation'. In its overwrought, stoned conversations, it is a dramatisation of moral opposites, as when Quentin and the American Marvell chat about sex. Quentin regrets juvenile promiscuity:

'When are these promiscuous tots going to put in time on growing up? When will their sexual emotions have time to develop? When will their natures have time to absorb frustration, yearning, joy, surprise —?'

'Christ, Quentin,' said Marvell, 'you trying to reinstitute sex-angst or what? Know who you sound like? Fuckin D. H. Lawrence! "Sexual emotions" – fuck them. Sex is something your body does, like eating or shitting. Yeah, like shitting. Just something your body does.'

An expression of weary decisiveness overcame Quentin's superb features. 'Well, it's not something *my* body does for me . . .'

This is mightily rudimentary, but mightily effective. 'Babies,' Marvell mutters, when Quentin declares himself 'in love', 'Dead, dead babies.' Fabulist, moralist . . . Amis is perhaps most obviously a parodist, a writer who submits everything, every character, every emotion, to heartless, supercharged burlesque as a means of achieving his effects. The most common criticism one hears levelled at *Money* is that it is 'way over the top' or 'unreal'. Both these criticisms are accurate to a degree, but there is a sense in which the excess and the 'unreality' are justified, authenticated, by the subject matter. After all, what is Amis writing about? *Money* is a frenzied account of a film director heading backwards and forwards across the Atlantic, led here and there into deals and celluloid fantasies by an associate, who, the novel finally reveals, has set the entire thing up. There is no money. There is no 'Fielding Goodney', Self's partner: he emerges as a vengeful woman in drag. The plot is actually a grotesque practical joke at Self's expense. By way of it Amis manages to expose the frailty of the mechanisms which bind our lives together here in the late 20th century, in this brave new Anglo-American world of ours. When it ends Self acknowledges that the premises on which he built his life were non-existent. Even his father wasn't his father. You could charge Amis – you could charge Carey – with being endlessly manipulative of their characters, but you could not accuse them of evading the mighty 'issues' with which the novelist has always wanted to contend. Carey is attempting to give his country a context. Amis is trying to dramatise the *dislocation* of much of modern life. 1930s Australia, where a truth is hardly separable from a lie, 1980s London and New York, in which nearly all motivation is built on deceit. As situations, these are not assimilable by the conventional tricks of the English novel. Both *Illywhacker* and *Money* in their distinctive ways are novels which emerge out of the conviction that 'reality' is in itself unreal. No conventional form can deal with Carey's outback or Amis's New York. Their novels might be larger than life, but they are responding to a complexity of circumstance which is similarly overblown.

With all this talk of 'complexity of circumstance', of writers unable to deal with the society they inhabit, it is very easy to forget the achievements of a group of older British writers who have consistently sought to tackle these luminous 'issues', if by way of trusted, conventional means. There is a depressing tendency to overlook writers like David Cook, who has written a string of novels about the voiceless underbelly of the subnormal and abused, or Piers Paul Read, who supplies a more formal perspective on one aspect, or one echelon, of 1970s and 1980s British society. Read, in particular, has been consistently under-rated; his reputation still skulking in that curious no-man's-land that lies between the rave review and sustained critical attention. Each of his book jackets comes spangled with flattering notice, telling you, say, that *The Villa Golitsyn* (1982) is 'an exhilarating novel, powerfully observed and provocatively written', but you could search for hours among those compendious articles about 'Developments in English Fiction' which occasionally decorate the highbrow papers and not find so much as the mention of his name. Probably this neglect has something to do with the author's oddly old-fashioned preoccupations. For Read – a queer thing in this secular age – is a religious, specifically Catholic writer.

Monk Dawson (1969), perhaps the most interesting of his early books, is about a well-intentioned priest who loses his vocation. *A Married Man* (1980) in its later stages is nothing less than a discussion of, well, sin. This does not mean that Read produces arch cheer-up stuff or the self-satisfied apologetics that have always disfigured 'religious' writing. *A Married Man*, for instance, the story of a barrister caught in that cliché of a plot, the mid-life crisis, is a desperately sad book, quite unrelenting in its effects. I can remember reading it at twenty and thinking that if this were middle age, then it might be better to stop while one still had the chance.

The second classic Read preoccupation is class. *The Upstart* (1973) is a deceptively simple tale of the revenge extracted by a middle-class vicar's son from the family of the local baronet. *A Married Man* is shot through with questions of position and status, and nearly every Read novel has its lurking snob aristocrat waiting to have the ground slashed away from beneath him. Yet these themes, atavisms almost, exist only as a backdrop to much wider concerns. Typically a Read novel moves into gear only when its chief character, having hitherto existed in a haze of cheery complacency, reaches out to grasp the question 'What are we to do with ourselves?' (the quotation is from *A Married Man*). So the professor in *The Professor's Daughter* realises that the influence he is supposed to exert on a US senator is both negligible and misguided. Strickland, the barrister, finds his life weirdly transformed by a chance encounter with a volume of Tolstoy. By linking these personal crises to broader political questions Read manages to bring off profound 'state of the nation' novels, such as *A Married Man*, set in the strike-bound English winter of 1973–4, or *The Professor's Daughter*, his 'American novel', which might be described as an exposé of liberalism, a political version of a book like *Dead Babies*. *A Season in the West*, his most recent novel, is another refinement of this technique. If nothing else, it shows a novelist writing about the City of London and actually seeming to know something about it.

There is much more to Read's fiction than this: the plausibility, the ability to write dialogue, the skill at introducing all manner of sensational events – murders, assassination attempts and whatnot – without the reader lifting an eyebrow. Given all these flash attributes it is worth asking why Read is not a really great novelist, why the reflection is distorted, and the answer lies in the easy solutions produced by the Catholicism. *The Upstart*, which might have been a fine, grim little tale, ends on a false, redemptive note when Hilary Fletcher strolls into a confession box. Then there is his characters' effortless, suspicious facility at getting things done, such as Hilary suddenly making large amounts of money or Strickland's becoming a Labour MP almost by picking up a telephone. Even realism demands its own subterfuges these days.

A novel like *A Married Man* is in some ways a direct response to a political situation, a book in which the hero engages formally in the political process. The formal, fictional examination of political processes is increasingly rare. A Snovian analysis of power, the perspective of a Trollope, would be impossible to construct. How does a novelist 'deal' with Mrs Thatcher or third-term Conservatism, how can he or she assimilate the mosaic of interests and random impetuses by which Britain is currently administered? In any case, it is arguable that the consequences rather than the processes provide the more fertile fictional soil: the most successful contemporary 'political' novels are informal texts, in which a character's inner confusions are seen to harbour broader political implications. Kelman's *A Disaffection* (1989) is a striking example of this approach: a novel not unlike Orwell's *Keep the Aspidistra Flying* in its assumption that a political creed is often a rationalisation of an emotional problem. Kelman's hero is Patrick Doyle, a twenty-nine-year-old Glasgow schoolteacher, terminally disillusioned, trapped in an existence of wayside indignities and sexual frustration, who sees himself as 'a tool . . . a fellow who received a greater than average wage for the business of fencing in the children of the suppressed poor'. The novel, written in a jagged stream-of-consciousness, is a lens held over a week in Doyle's life: a week of hard, joyless drinking, tetchy common-room chat, and the eerie sprightliness that tracks a mind at the end of its tether. 'Now weans,' Doyle addresses his class, 'I am demanding a bit of order, a bit of order, otherwise I'm closing the pub early. Okay! Right: open your fucking jotters and get scribbling.' The eerie, sonorous vocal style, half playful, half desperate, is characteristic: aping the casual rhythms of speech even in its narrative accounts of Doyle's thought processes and its slammed-home obscenities:

> Yes, the faces are smiling. The wee first-years are good. Maybe they are Patrick's favourite group. Just at the age they are approaching teenagehood. He seems to have an okay relationship with them. I'm chucking this job in because I want to play the pipes. But these pipes have got fuck all to do with Scotland. Does anyone know the term 'fugisticism'? And dont answer too fast because I dont think the term has existed before the last five minutes. So there you are, that's the way things are, how ye can just fucking walk in here and invent your own terms. I've got my own terms and so have you. You've just got to make sure they're no yours . . .

This is an authentic style, a *working-class style*, not using words in a way that implies a middle-class value judgement. When Kelman uses a bourgeois cliché he draws attention to it, inserts a set of invisible punctuation marks, to let you know that it's a bourgeois cliché. On one level this is Scots realism, not unlike the work of William McIllvanney, whose novels use a series of obvious metaphors to suggest the weakening influences at work on Scots culture. But again, that eclecticism – a sheaf of reference points from far away, from Kafka, Kierkegaard and Hölderlin, and the weird sending up of stock situations, such as the occasion when Doyle imagines that the fish on the plate before him is talking: 'Just please devour me,

I'm as good as the next thing you'll catch. Whatever you do dont not do it, dont not devour me. I'm a good wee fish . . .' Even the solemnity of the political message – what remote, southern Conservatism has done to Scotland – is consistently undermined in this way. Doyle instructs his class to repeat after him:

> We are being fenced in by the teachers
> We are being fenced in by the teachers
> at the behest of a dictatorship government
> at the behest of a dictatorship government
> in explicit simulation of our fucking parents the silly
>   bastards
> in explicit simulation of our fucking parents the silly
>   bastards
> Laughter.

Doyle has his moments of transient release: watching football, visiting his brother's family, and wild, crazy schemes for eloping to England with a married colleague. But the relationship with Alison escapes him and in a Kafkaesque scene he discovers that he is being transferred to another school as the result of an application he doesn't remember submitting. The novel ends with him drunk, chasing taxis in the rain. *A Disaffection* is a mad, embittered book, invested with an anger that usually eludes the formal cadences of the drawing-room novel. Its ultimate effect is to denote a symbiosis between emotional and political feeling. Gordon Comstock's surly anarchism might have seemed to be the result of some emotional fracture. With Doyle there is the suggestion of a complex relationship between a personal turmoil and a political landscape. Life, just as much as art, is propaganda and Kelman provides a convincing display of the ideology of an individual's interior life.

An individual, it ought to be said, cunningly overseen by his creator. There is a self-awareness about some of Kelman's narrators which is a consequence of the type of fictional

framework he operates within. Kelman without the intellectual architecture, without the *relentlessness*, would not be a
great distance away from Pat Barker, whose novels about the
North-East of England – notably *Union Street* (1982) and
Blow Your House Down (1984) – show a similar preoccupation with the problems of an authentic style. With Barker,
again, there is the concern to establish a prose which reflects
'ordinary' speech. Brenda in *Blow Your House Down* is the
subject of a typical reminiscence: 'Even before they were
married he'd thought nothing of hitting her if she didn't have
his shirts ironed. But she was pregnant and his nerves were
bad and she thought Oh, well, it'll be different when we're
married. It was. He hit her harder.' The irony is characteristic.
A novel specifically concerned with violence against women,
an extrapolation of the Yorkshire Ripper case, *Blow Your
House Down* is not afraid to reach for the occasional symbolic
height. So Brenda, taking a wrong turning in the meat-packing
factory, ends up on the killing-room floor. 'Oh you don't go
in there,' a shocked supervisor tells her. 'Killing's for the
men.' While the voice is not always consistently maintained,
the novel's descriptive passages – the murder of Kath the
prostitute – are frighteningly intense, its urban landscapes
bleakly evoked.

Landscape. All of Kelman's work – the short stories collected in *Greyhound for Breakfast*, for instance – is deeply
rooted in environment, in *A Disaffection* it is Glasgow and
its West of Scotland fringe, even if the pious absorption in
scene only exposes Doyle's own personal limitations. Sitting
in his car, vainly plotting escape, he realises that 'he'll never
get beyond the wider reaches of greater Glasgow'. Characteristically, the techniques of fable, myth, illusion, the magnifi-
cations of reality you see in a Carey or a Martin Amis, achieve
their sharpest focus in writing about place, novels in which
individual lives are linked inexorably with environment. Kelman's fellow Scot Alasdair Gray does this in *Lanark* (1981).
In *Waterland* (1983) Graham Swift stamps an ulterior connection on myth and landscape. Crick, his seedy school teacher,

stuck in front of a silent class, busily analyses his Cambridge-shire childhood:

> To live in the Fens is to receive strong doses of reality. The great, flat monotony of reality; the wide, empty space of reality. Melancholia and self-murder are not unknown in the Fens. Heavy drinking, madness and sudden acts of violence are not uncommon. How do you surmount reality, children? How do you acquire, in a flat country, the tonic of elevated feelings?
>
> How did the Cricks outwit reality? By telling stories. Down to the last generation, they were not only phleg-matic but superstitious and credulous creatures. Suckers for stories. While the Atkinsons made history, the Cricks spun yarns.

Waterland is an attempt to 'outwit reality'. Our appreciation of the past, it suggests, rests on its falsification. 'There are times,' Crick observes, 'when we have to disentangle history from fairy-tale. Let us get back to solid ground.' However, the final effect of the novel is to demonstrate that this is impossible. There is no solid ground: the 'waterland' of Crick's childhood is as dislocated as his adult life. Crick's world is beginning to dissolve. His headmaster, a snuffy little peda-gogue who imagines that history is somehow of less practical value than physics, wants to close his department. His wife, having taken up religion, begins to act strangely, particularly over the tragedy of her childlessness, eventually purloining an infant from its pram outside a supermarket. Crick's response to all this and to the nagging of a pupil, one of those irritating boys who turn history lessons into a discussion of the value of historical study, is to abandon any attempt to teach and tell his class the story of his childhood: 'a fairy tale ... but then we lived in a fairy-tale world.'

Consequently, Swift's novel exists on several planes. On one hand it is an example of middle-age crisis, on another that rare thing a decent regional novel, on a third a profound discussion of the historical process and its relevance. 'Stuff the past,' says Master Price to Crick. But you cannot stuff the past, as the study of Crick's formative years and their incidental tragedies reveals. *Waterland* is a fine example of an ancient genre – the regional novel has been in shoddy disrepute since the days of Hugh Walpole – revivified. A similar ability to surmount staider conventions emerges in the work of the Cumbrian novelist John Murray. Murray's two novels, *Samarkand* (1985) and *Kin* (1986), differ very little in theme and treatment. Underlying *Samarkand* is an adroit, lurking determinism that anchors family life in a regional context, in this case the tiny strip of West Cumbria from Whitehaven up to the Solway, and pushes it forward with no very great impetus. *Kin*, while drawing out the theme of family relationships, has a similar grounding in 'the unique shabby distinction of the fading industrial belt along the Solway Firth'.

Samarkand is a sort of poetic meditation on the way in which people regard their environment. *Kin*, the better novel, might be described as a meditation on the family in time, and if that sounds unalluring, it ought to be said that an occasional heaviness of exposition is constantly redeemed by the author's capricious sense of humour. The family at the centre of *Kin* are the idiosyncratic Demesnes, and the strength of the ties that bind them is made plain from the opening scene in which James Demesne and his grandson sun themselves on a 1950s Cumbrian beach. Baby James is the axis on which family history turns, a link between a dense, receding past and an uncertain future. A little further on into the book James, sitting guard on his own infant nephew, listens to the baby howling 'and with that cry James felt himself for the first time bounded by a love of kin, a rarity of feeling indeed ... of belly to belly between kind and kin'. Though the remainder of the book unfurls James's career to early manhood, from schoolboy prodigy to undergraduate bohemian and unpublished writer, the thread endures; a complex web of feeling with an unhappy final twist.

This ungainly process is described by a series of minute,

documentary techniques, patient evocations of scene – Mazo de la Roche from the library, the Pretty Things on the radio, an obsession with forgotten brands of cigarettes – and, it must be said, an absence of all but the most perfunctory of plots. The key, once more, is language. Murray achieves his best touches by means of a kind of learned, oxymoronical slang. So James Demesne, frolicking on the beach with his grandson, slides 'a hearty tablet of ice-cream' into the infant's 'negligible maw'. The imagery is firmly rooted in the environment it is trying to define. While one character 'sways like a hinged gate' another 'starts like a bantam on one leg', a device which transcends simple comedy and chains people to their milieu by the sheer power of the language. *Kin* is a number of things: a novel about social change, an *éducation sentimentale* of the 1960s. Technically it is a novel of stylistic variety. There is a blatancy about its continuities and a relish about its incidental detail which makes you suspect that in the best experimental tradition Murray distrusts plot and, by constantly frustrating the reader with sneaky, determinist hints, wants to abolish suspense. On the other hand there is the celebration of human-ism, a ceremonious absorption in the fucking, eating and farting side of human life which, despite its occasional traged-ies, ends on an up. 'The night after he had made love to his wife Demesne pondered secretly the welfare of his departed nephew and after dreaming of sundry mansions he awoke with certain hopes.' It is a conception that owes more to the 18th century than to cannier modern stylists: a recreation of past life which achieves coherence because of an intensity of feeling. Whatever the stylistic conflation, however determinist the conceit, at heart it is still the single, humane intelligence which remains, and will always remain, at the novel's core.

'May we have imagination instead of politics, aspiration in-stead of history,' Malcolm Bradbury once declared during the course of a wary interview in *The Times*. This seems to me to be a confusion of fictional means and ends. The novel *is* politics in that it is an analysis, a reflection, a refraction of prevailing circumstance. All that is in doubt is the novelist's ability to contend with this vast, constantly shifting chaos of circumstance, an undertaking in which the old, formal methods are more or less useless. Only 'imagination', fakery, illusion, conflated styles, Carey's enlivening lies, can match up to the demands of this random, shifting landscape. The 'commitment' of the writers under discussion here is not one of political orthodoxy — Kelman is a socialist, most of the others accept the liberal package in one way or another — but a willingness to engage, to regard the novel as a worthwhile vehicle to examine the issues of individual and communal experience here at the fag-end of the 20th century. This might seem an elevated conception for something whose primary duty is merely to entertain, but it is something the great fiction has always done. Consequently, as much as *Vanity Fair* or *Dombey and Son* or whatever, the key texts of the 1980s are 'political' books. *Money*, for instance, is one of the first novels to appreciate the fact that we inhabit not so much an English or a Western as an *Anglo-American* society. *A Disaffection* might be described as an essay in frustrated humanism. And what is frustrating Kelman's humanism, what in the last instance has made life scarcely worth living? In the context of modern Scotland, with its urban wasteland and its political denaturing, this hardly needs spelling out.

To single out this handful of conspicuous stylists is wildly invidious. It ignores the achievements of a variety of other writers: a 'womanist' school containing voices as diverse as Lorna Tracy or the late Sarah Baylis, for instance; or at the other end of the scale a group of loosely affiliated gay male writers ranging from Adam Mars-Jones to Simon Burt. But to isolate the distinction of a novel like *Money* or *Illywhacker* is to disguise, partially, a sprawling landscape of underachievement. Not that one should attribute blame. The odds are stacked against the serious writer, perhaps more obviously than ever before. No adequate critical forum exists in which he can usefully participate. At every juncture a group of idle cultural saboteurs will rise up to accuse him of 'cleverness'.

There is in any case an increasing public disregard for whatever it is that he is trying to do. More enervating even than this is the imposition on him by his critics, whether he likes it or not, of quietism. For still in this country for a novelist to engage with political reality, for Martin Amis, say, to publish a collection of short stories about the Bomb, is to uncork a torrent of nonsense to the effect that it is the novelist's duty somehow to 'be above' politics. The consequence of this attitude is that for most novelists the choice seems to lie between trying to write the type of book, the witless panorama, that can't be written these days, or slumbering on 'inside the whale' in Orwell's lustrous phrase. To rest supine in the wide, comforting darkness is an agreeable position, but it is not something you can do in the late 1980s. Mrs Thatcher. The European single market. The Bomb. Fundamentalist Islam. Whatever one may feel about them, they are not something you can ignore, not any more, and the writer who does so is simply not a functioning part of the world. It is time to step outside. Not perhaps to picket-lines, demonstrations or any of those events at which the presence of a few middle-aged novelists and literary gentlewomen is such an embarrassment, but *outside* – out on to bare, level plains of warring armies and mighty clangour from which art retreated so long ago.

Appendix

Forty from the 1980s

A selection of the best British and Commonwealth fiction from the period 1980–1989.

PETER ACKROYD, *The Last Testament of Oscar Wilde* (1983, Hamish Hamilton hb, Abacus pb)

PETER ACKROYD, *Hawksmoor* (1984, Hamish Hamilton hb, Abacus pb)

MARTIN AMIS, *Money* (1984, Jonathan Cape hb, Penguin pb)

MARTIN AMIS, *Einstein's Monsters* (1987, Jonathan Cape hb, Penguin pb)

MARGARET ATWOOD, *The Handmaid's Tale* (1986, Jonathan Cape hb, Virago pb)

J. G. BALLARD, *Hello America* (1981, Jonathan Cape hb, Granada pb)

JULIAN BARNES, *Flaubert's Parrot* (1984, Jonathan Cape hb, Picador pb)

PAT BARKER, *Union Street* (1982, Virago hb and pb)

PAT BARKER, *Blow Your House Down* (1984, Virago hb and pb)

SARAH BAYLIS, *Utrillo's Mother* (1987, Pandora Press hb)

NEIL BISSOONDATH, *Digging up the Mountain* (1986, André Deutsch hb, Penguin pb)

JOHN BRODERICK, *The Flood* (1987, Marion Boyars hb)

A. S. BYATT, *Still Life* (1985, Chatto & Windus hb, Penguin pb)

PETER CAREY, *Illywhacker* (1985, Faber hb and pb)

J. L. CARR, *A Month in the Country* (1980, Harvester Press hb, Penguin pb)

ANGELA CARTER, *Nights at the Circus* (1984, Chatto & Windus hb, Picador pb)

BRUCE CHATWIN, *On the Black Hill* (1982, Jonathan Cape hb, Picador pb)

MAX EGREMONT, *The Ladies' Man* (1983, Secker & Warburg hb)

ALASDAIR GRAY, *Lanark* (1981, Canongate hb, Picador pb)

ALASDAIR GRAY/JAMES KELMAN/AGNES OWENS, *Lean Tales* (1985, Jonathan Cape hb, Abacus pb)

ROY HEATH, *The Shadow Bride* (1987, Collins hb, Flamingo pb)

KAZURO ISHIGURO, *An Artist of the Floating World* (1986, Faber hb and pb)

NEIL JORDAN, *The Past* (1980, Jonathan Cape hb, Abacus pb)

JAMES KELMAN, *Greyhound for Breakfast* (1987, Secker & Warburg hb, Picador pb)

JAMES KELMAN, *A Disaffection* (1989, Secker & Warburg hb)

DAVID LODGE, *How Far Can You Go?* (1980, Secker & Warburg hb, Penguin pb)

IAN MCEWAN, *The Child in Time* (1987, Jonathan Cape hb, Picador pb)

WILLIAM MCILLVANNEY, *The Big Man* (1985, Hodder & Stoughton hb, Sceptre pb)

TIMOTHY MO, *Sour/Sweet* (1982, André Deutsch hb, Abacus pb)

ALICE MUNRO, *The Moons of Jupiter* (1983, Allen Lane hb, Penguin pb)

JOHN MURRAY, *Kin* (1986, Aidan Ellis hb)

SHIVA NAIPAUL, *A Hot Country* (1983, Hamish Hamilton hb, Abacus pb)

PIERS PAUL READ, *A Married Man* (1980, The Alison Press hb, Pan pb)

PIERS PAUL READ, *A Season in the West* (1988, The Alison Press hb)

SALMAN RUSHDIE, *Midnight's Children* (1981, Jonathan Cape hb, Picador pb)

GRAHAM SWIFT, *Learning to Swim and other stories* (1982, London Magazine Editions hb, Picador pb)

GRAHAM SWIFT, *Waterland* (1983, Heinemann hb, Picador pb)

COLIN THUBRON, *A Cruel Madness* (1985, Heinemann hb, Penguin pb)

WILLIAM TREVOR, *Fools of Fortune* (1983, Bodley Head hb, Penguin pb)

JEANNETTE WINTERSON, *The Passion* (1987, Bloomsbury hb, Penguin pb)